CO-AWJ-455

# MULTICULTURALISM IN ACADEME

SOURCE BOOKS ON EDUCATION
VOLUME 47
GARLAND REFERENCE LIBRARY OF SOCIAL SCIENCE
VOLUME 980

# MULTICULTURALISM IN ACADEME
## A SOURCE BOOK

LIBBY V. MORRIS
SAMMY PARKER

GARLAND PUBLISHING, INC.
NEW YORK AND LONDON
1996

378.199
M877m

**Library of Congress Cataloging-in-Publication Data**

Morris, Libby V.
  Multiculturalism in academe : a source book / by Libby V. Morris,
Sammy Parker.
    p.    cm. — (Garland reference library of social science ; vol. 980.
Source books on education ; vol. 47)
    Includes bibliographical references (p.     ) and index.
    ISBN 0-8153-1798-0 (alk. paper)
    1. Education, Higher—United States—Curricula.   2. Multicultural edu-
cation—United States.   3. Minorities—Education (Higher)—United States.
4. Political correctness—United States.   I. Parker, Sammy.   II. Title.
III. Series: Garland reference library of social science ; v. 980.   IV. Series:
Garland reference library of social science.   Source books on education ;
vol. 47.
LB2361.5.M68   1996
378.199'0973—dc20                                                    95–26398
                                                                        CIP

Printed on acid-free, 250-year-life paper
Manufactured in the United States of America

# CONTENTS

# INTRODUCTION TO MULTICULTURALISM

How multicultural are the curricula of higher education? Have changing student demographics and the newer forms of scholarship transformed the academy? These questions are not easily answered although even the casual observer of higher education will recognize that much has changed, from who is on campus to what they are studying. This manuscript, then, grew out of a need to understand better the changes in the curricula of higher education over the last two decades and to make articles and books describing these shifts accessible to colleagues and students, both within and outside academe.

Much of the recent change in higher education, both in academics and demographics, may be attributed to the civil rights movement of the 1960s and the social and political unrest sweeping the nation at that time. Antiwar marches, minority and women's rights, student protests, and demands for a relevant curriculum dominated the agenda of higher education. The assassination of Martin Luther King, Jr., and the shootings at Kent State and Jackson State also had far-reaching impact on the agenda — educational and otherwise — of the nation in the following years. Throughout the 1960s and 1970s questions of gender, class, race, and ethnicity grew in importance in American society. In higher education, access and equity became central questions of concern, and, concurrently, a new generation of scholars and students, mainly women and minorities, was beginning to ask questions of the canon, its authors and subjects.

The interest in the contents of the canon — who was taught and what was taught — was largely supported by shifts in demographics; enrollments increased overall, and women and minority participation grew in record numbers, a change that frequently is cited as one of the major social shifts in the last half of the twentieth century. In 1960 higher education in the United States was largely the domain of white male students and faculty. Of the 4.8 million college students in 1964, only 1.8 million were women and even fewer were minorities. By 1992, however, women were in the majority (55%), having reached that plateau in 1987, and minorities represented 20% of the 14.5 million college students nationwide. Between 1982 and 1992, enrollment by African Americans, the nation's largest minority group, increased from approximately 1.1 million to 1.4 million overall (Almanac Issue, 1994).

The increases in minority participation in higher education reflect growing diversity in the population nationwide. Higher birth rates among people of color, increases in immigration from non-Western countries, and a higher median age overall in the white population result in a more heterogeneous school population, workforce, and nation (Banks, 1991; Morris, 1994; Levine, 1989; American Council on Education, 1988). Educational reformers cite these changes as evidence of a demographic imperative for a more inclusive, multicultural education (Banks, 1991).

## Connections and Diversity

Women's studies, along with African-American studies, ethnic studies, and global studies, is fundamentally interdisciplinary. All of these areas ask questions and seek answers that cross disciplinary boundaries. At the center of multicultural research and teaching are questions of race, gender, ethnicity, and class. The reformers within these studies challenge the social construction of "truth" and challenge the fundamental claim of "objectivity," the foundation of traditional inquiry. Thus, the newer scholarship challenges traditional knowledge and the knowledge producers. The "multiculturalists" seek recognition for difference, for multiple perspectives, and for the reality thus created, which is distinct yet inherently related to other perspectives and senses of "reality." This scholarship attempts to make students aware of how their historical and cultural positions are "connected to and different from" those experiences of people from other places and times (Schmitz, 1992).

In the 1960s, concomitant with social and political unrest in general, women and minorities began to question with increasing frequency and decibel the monocultural view of the academy, a perspective characterized as white, male, and Eurocentric; thus began the long and continuing process that brought emerging cultural, racial, and feminist perspectives to academe. At the same time, many of the reformers began to question the concept of objectivity in traditional scholarship and in the canon and to regard an unquestioning loyalty to claims of objectivity as only a defense of the status quo. The reformers argue that when the experiences of white males are used as references to judge all other people, the "other" are relegated to inferior status and, often, invisibility. If this premise is accepted, conclusions based on traditional methodological errors perpetuate myths about the lives and experiences of the people who are not the norm.

Multicultural education is not "one thing" or one activity or one program; it is new courses and revised ones — cross-listed and interdisciplinary; it is certificate programs and degree programs; it is women's centers and African-American centers; it is area studies and ethnic studies and studies of ageism, sexism, sexual orientation, and classism. It is a continuous process in education to address both diversity and connection. It seeks not only to correct and add, but also to redesign curricular and research paradigms (O'Barr, 1994).

## Black Studies

Leading the way in curricular change in colleges and universities were studies by and about African Americans (Butler, 1991). Black studies grew out of the political movements of the 1960s and 1970s concurrent with the rapid increase in the number of black students and faculty on college campuses and African Americans in the workplaces of industry, social services, and government (Cole, 1991). Black studies asserts that the social concepts developed by white Americans and Europeans do not adequately describe, and are inconsistent with, the social and cultural realities faced by most black people; therefore, in addition to the creation and dissemination of new scholarship, one of the most salient purposes of black studies is "to effect social, political and economic change" (Anderson, 1993, p. 45).   The first black or African-American studies department was started at San Francisco State in 1968 (Anderson, 1993). African-American students quickly noticed the lack of any curricular treatment of Africans in American higher education, and this observation stirred campus activity. The intensity spread to Stanford, Cornell, and Ohio State, among others, and these universities became involved in curricular change, recruitment of black students, employment of black faculty, and concern with other relevant issues.

Note that "black studies" is a generic term and there is an ongoing debate over nomenclature; some prefer "Afro-American," others, "African and Afro-American" or "Africana" studies (Hine, 1990). Additionally, "ethnic studies" has come to serve as an umbrella term for Asian American Studies, black studies, American Indian Studies, and Latino studies (Butler, 1991). This variety in program nomenclature effectively characterizes the diversity in programs on traditionally white and historically black campuses nationwide.

The oldest of these studies, Africana studies, dates its beginning from the 1890s with an attempt to document and analyze the history, status, and culture of African peoples. The second stage of Africana study was the study of black America, regarded by some as a setback based on the resultant methodologies and conclusions. The civil rights movement then brought about a third stage in Africana studies, during which white institutions were more willing to establish Africana programs, if not departments. The research paradigm in these programs shifted from Eurocentrism to Afrocentrism. The interest was in the lives of black Americans and a corresponding push to analyze and interpret that experience in context using an Afrocentric lens, as opposed to a comparative one that uses the European standard. Legitimization and institutionalization were reached in phase three. Africana studies was then well on its way to phase four, to broaden and refine the field of inquiry (Harris, 1990).

Over the past three decades, questions of race became central in the emerging African-American scholarship. By the early 1970s, an estimated 800 black studies programs and departments existed nationwide. Subsequently, a decline in the number of programs followed for a variety of reasons: for example, loss of political momentum, funding cuts, the failure of many black faculty to gain tenure, white and black apathy, and the struggle to establish legitimacy. According to the National Council for Black Studies, approximately 375 programs were in existence in 1991 (Cole, 1991).

African-American studies shares with women's studies its peripheral location in the academy. Like ethnic studies, both were administrative responses to pressures from women and minorities. Most often, the scholars shared the characteristics under study, whether race or gender, unlike the scholars in area studies and other disciplines. Women's studies and ethnic studies also have relied on a variety of financial arrangements for survival, as institutional support and governmental support often would rise and fall subject to the viewpoints of those in power (Musil and Sales, 1991). Significant financial support for these interdisciplinary fields, however, has come from outside the academy from private foundations, corporations, and individuals (Bolland and Walter, 1991). Through its financial assistance — over $20 million between 1969 and 1990 alone — the Ford Foundation has been instrumental in supporting both undergraduate and graduate work and research in black studies (Harris, 1990).

In the last decade of the twentieth century, African-American studies continues to become stronger as an interdisciplinary field with a growing number of graduates and an increase in the number of related scholarly journals and professional organizations. One significant challenge to the field, as is true in women's studies, is to continue the drive to recruit young students in the wake of vocationalism and professional study that has overtaken students and courses of study in higher education.

## Women's Studies

Women's studies grew out of the women's movement of the 1960s and 1970s and the awareness by women faculty and students of what they perceived as the monocultural perspective of the academy, where women and minorities were invisible in content and research (National Women's Studies Association, 1991). Underlying the development of this prominent new area of study were two key premises: (1) gender matters in cultural, historical, and social analysis and (2) inequality between the sexes, as a human construction rather than a divine or natural ordinance, is a necessary subject for social, cultural, and historical analysis (Miller and Treitel, 1991). And, of course, one major goal of women's studies was, and continues to be, curricular transformation.

Peggy McIntosh (1983) developed an analysis of the phases of curricular change as feminist perspectives emerged in the new scholarship. In phase one, the "womanless" phase, the absence of women is noted, and highly exclusionary standards for inclusion are upheld. In phase two, the search for women commences, using the same male-centered perspective and ideas, and the "women in" courses and research are developed. In phase three, women are viewed as problems or an anomaly when judged by androcentric standards. These studies portray women and minorities as deficient, and these perspectives launched the search for a feminist paradigm (phase four) where women and their issues are central, measured against their own values, concerns, and behaviors — women on their own terms. Phase five, still to be achieved, McIntosh (1983) advances, is "lateral consciousness" where the interests of all may be served without subordination of another. In a similar vein, Schuster and VanDyne (1985) describe curriculum change as moving from an invisibility of women, to identifying sexism in traditional knowledge, to searching for missing women, to conceptualizing women as a subordinate group, and then to studying women on their own terms.

The first women's studies program was formally approved at San Diego State University in 1970. At about the same time on the East Coast, a women's studies program was developing at Cornell University (Chamberlain, 1994). In 1977 the National Women's Studies Association was formed, and 276 programs were identified nationwide. The growth continued: in 1987 there were approximately 500 programs, and according to the National Women's Studies Association, in 1990 there were 621 women's studies programs offering certificates or degrees nationwide (Musil, 1992).

Most important to the growth of women's studies was the development of centers for research on women. Once again, the Ford Foundation played a significant part in the development, and the first centers were started in 1974 at Stanford University and Wellesley College (Chamberlain, 1994). Others were soon to follow these models. Presently, the National Council for Research on Women, founded in 1981 in New York, serves as an independent association of 75 centers and organizations that focus on feminist research, policy analysis, and educational programs for women and girls.

Women's studies also was aided by the development of subcommittees and commissions within the professional associations of the established academic disciplines. Among the first were committees established by the American Historical Association and the Modern Language Association. These groups promoted women, their issues, and feminist research. Formed in

1988, the National Council for Research on Women's National Network of Women's Caucuses is a coalition of over 200 caucuses, commissions, and groups in the academic disciplines and professional associations. In a similar vein, the Association of American Colleges, Project on the Status and Education of Women, founded in 1971, acts as a liaison between various groups, develops materials that identify issues important to women's achievement, monitors federal statutes and policies, and provides policy analysis of issues concerning women in higher education.

The development of over 40 feminist presses and numerous professional journals in women's studies has advanced further the field of study. Additionally, since 1980 over 200 curriculum integration projects have occurred nationwide (National Women's Studies Association, 1991). Many of these efforts would not have developed without the strong involvement of funding agencies and philanthropies such as the Ford Foundation, the Fund for the Improvement of Postsecondary Education, and the Mott Foundation.

Presently, women's studies is a fully institutionalized part of higher education, both as a discipline and as an interdisciplinary field; yet much work remains to widen the presence, especially in two-year and community colleges, historically black institutions, and private traditional colleges (Hatton, 1994). The growth internationally, however, is impressive, evidenced by the forums and conferences across Europe and in Canada that include feminist scholars and women's programs from industrialized and developing nations (Howe, 1994).

A survey of the literature also highlights the dynamic quality of women's studies programs and the presence of internal tensions that remain to be confronted. For example, in the 1980s women of color began to question women's studies and curriculum integration projects for their inattention to differences in race, class, gender, and culture. The fundamental issue was captured by the title *All the Women Are White, All the Blacks Are Men, But Some of Us Are Brave: Black Women's Studies* (Hull, Scott, and Smith, 1982). The phrase "women of color" captured the essence of the concern that femaleness was not a monolithic category and that race/ethnicity should be conceptualized beyond the dichotomy of black and white. A clarion call issued forth that an emerging, more holistic epistemology was on the horizon, one that examined more fully the intersection of race and gender and class/cultural differences.

## Change in the Academy

Curricular change in the academy is not limited to women's studies or black studies. Questions of race, gender, and class — issues at the core of multicultural research and teaching — may be asked in any discipline; consequently, the literature descriptive of multicultural change in higher education derives from two major sources: traditional disciplines and newer fields and interdisciplinary areas.

Women's studies, for example, refuses to be bound by the departmentalization that disciplines impose on themselves. Women's studies is interdisciplinary and holistic. Students are encouraged to go beyond the discrete subjects of study and learn from the experiences in their own lives (Wetzel, 1993). Thus, women's studies draws methods and materials from a variety of disciplines and develops new approaches in pedagogy and research addressing issues of gender, race, and class.

The same is true of other studies, for instance, African American, Native American, and Hispanic. Thus, the growing influence of these studies implies a powerful impetus for a number of changes within the academy. The birth and growth of areas that have been even more marginalized — such as gay and lesbian studies — increase significantly the forces for change that began in earnest in the 1960s.

## Organization

This bibliography includes works descriptive of multiculturalism's impact on college and university curricula during the 1980s and early 1990s. Included are writings that address changes in both the traditional disciplines and the emerging fields, for example, women's studies, African-American studies, and ethnic studies. The emphasis is on the curricula of higher education — what is taught, broadly defined, and why. Prominent are articles that address curricular change across the academy and at the disciplinary level. Many articles focus on integrating the emerging scholarship into introductory courses and the core curriculum where newer perspectives have the potential for affecting the largest number of students.

Black studies and women's studies are most prominent in this collection. Newer areas of study (for example, Asian-American women's studies) are continuing to evolve, and their representation in the literature is quite limited. Hopefully, the newer areas can be explored more fully with the references provided. Excluded are writings that focus on the development of theories and specific content for courses and works that focus exclusively on pedagogy. Guides to the literature in these areas are included in the final chapter.

Chapter two, "Rationale," includes articles and books that attempt to define multiculturalism, both philosophically and demographically, and its effect on the academy. Included are writings from the "curricular crusades" that this movement has spawned over the past 15 years. Proponents on both sides and in the middle in this ongoing debate, along with their specific arguments for and against changing the curriculum, are represented. The debates are often contentious, and national personalities and faculty, both inside and outside academe, are included. Some of the better known writers include Allan Bloom, Lynne Cheney, George Will, and Johnnella Butler, moving from traditionalists to reformer.

Chapter three, "Institutional Case Studies," describes actual institutional experiences and shows the broad range of ways that higher education institutions of all types have been affected by the components of multiculturalism. The works annotated in this section describe institutional initiatives — purposes, impediments, activities, reactions, and results. The documented changes may affect entire universities and colleges, and in some cases, extend across states and/or regions. Also noteworthy is the involvement of philanthropic organizations, professional organizations, and other agencies in supporting and bringing about change. This section provides a useful guide to change at specific institutions.

Chapter four, "Traditional Disciplines and Interdisciplinary Fields," includes examples of specific, curricular change in the traditional disciplines and in the emerging fields. Examples of curriculum integration (i.e., adding new scholarship to existing courses) and curricular additions (i.e., adding new courses that examine issues of gender, race, and/or class) are included. In most cases, the rationales for such changes are included as part of the text, indicating that justification for the newer scholarship is still required in many fields and at many institutions. Although the annotations in chapters four and five suggest that curricular change is widespread and has affected many disciplines, the impact and depth of these changes are yet to be determined.

For the most part, the works described in the chapters are organized alphabetically by author; however, chapter four groups the works into several broad categories (e.g., African-American studies, anthropology, literature/English, and math/science). It is not suggested that these are the only works describing change in the traditional disciplines and interdisciplinary fields; no doubt, professional associations have internal publications developed by subsections and commissions that deal with changes in their respective disciplines. Rather, included herein are the articles that have made their way into the leading journals from the emerging fields and the older established disciplines. These writings are a useful guide to the issues at the disciplinary level, the nature of the changes, implementation strategies, and future needs.

Chapter five, "Evaluation and Assessment," presents actual quantitative and qualitative studies designed to measure the impact of multiculturalism in academe. For two decades the reformers have advocated change in the academy and designed and implemented curriculum-transformation projects. The case studies in chapter three and the reports from the disciplines in chapter four record the presence of change; they do not document the effectiveness or outcomes of these changes. Only recently have the emerging fields matured to the point of evaluation and assessment. And, perhaps in response to the growing concern nationally with student assessment, issues of effectiveness are beginning to be addressed and reported in the literature.

The interest in documentation of strengths, weaknesses, and outcomes shows maturing of the "emerging fields." While earlier surveys, like that done by the Association of American Colleges (Levine and Cureton, 1992), sought to document the extent of multicultural activities, more recent studies attempt to assess change systematically in students and in courses of study. For example, since 1992, four major studies emerging in women's studies have examined the areas of student outcomes (Luebke and

Reilly, 1995; Musil, 1992), changes in the disciplines (Zinsser, 1993), and program effectiveness (Musil, 1992).

Chapter six, "Political Correctness," examines the vitriol that is increasingly present on college campuses in discussions of issues such as employment, financial aid, admissions, and curricula. These wide-ranging attacks by the traditionalists on the reformers (and vice-versa) and their positions have coalesced under the term "political correctness." That is, reformers and their supporters are accused of responding to issues in a politically correct fashion rather than in academically or educationally sound ways. For some, the accusations likely are used to resist serious dialogue about important issues in the academy. Under this term, however, traditionalists from a wide range of disciplines have found a common thread to link and resist change.

Chapter seven, "Guide to Resources: Bibliographies and Reference Books," includes a wide range of bibliographies and reference books that serve as a guide to issues of concern to women and minorities. Included in this section are directories of programs, organizations, and resources, plus reference books for the education of specific populations (e.g., Chicano, Latino, and Hispanic). The proponents of multicultural education also describe paradigm shifts in pedagogy and research for the new scholarship.

Journals referenced in this bibliography are listed in the Appendix. An author index also is provided.

## Audience

Although we hope that this text will be useful to those in women's studies, ethnic studies, and fields with multicultural concerns, the intended audience is far wider. This book also should serve administrators who have to deal with demands for courses and programs and the funds to support them. It is intended to assist curriculum committees who have overworked faculty members and little time to go beyond their own campuses to look at challenges and change in curriculum. And it is intended for students studying in the academic field of higher education who will someday in a practical way be caught in addressing the questions of whom will we teach? what will we teach? why will we teach these things? and how?

*References*

"Almanac Issue." *The Chronicle of Higher Education* 41 (1) (September 1, 1994): 15.

American Council on Education and the Education Commission of the States. *One-Third of a Nation: A Report of the Commission on Minority Participation in Education and American Life*. Washington, DC: American Council on Education, 1988.

Anderson, Talmadge. *Introduction to African American Studies: Cultural Concepts and Theory*. Dubuque, IA: Kendall/Hunt Publishing Company, 1993.

Banks, James A. "Multicultural Literacy and Curriculum Reform." *Educational Horizons* 69 (3) (Spring 1991): 135-140.

Bolland, Katharine, and John C. Walter. "Private Foundation Grants to American Ethnic Studies Departments and Programs, 1972-1988: Patterns and Prospects." In *Transforming the Curriculum: Ethnic Studies and Women's Studies*, edited by Johnnella E. Butler and John C. Walter, 35-50. New York: State University of New York Press, Albany, 1991.

Butler, Johnnella E. "The Difficult Dialogue of Curriculum Transformation: Ethnic Studies and Women's Studies." In *Transforming the Curriculum: Ethnic Studies and Women's Studies*, edited by Johnnella E. Butler and John C. Walter, 1-19. New York: State University of New York Press, Albany, 1991.

Chamberlain, Mariam K. "Multicultural Women's Studies in the United States." *Women's Studies Quarterly* 22 (3 & 4) (Fall/Winter 1994): 215-225.

Cole, Johnnetta B. "Black Studies in Liberal Arts Education." In *Transforming the Curriculum: Ethnic Studies and Women's Studies*, edited by Johnnella E. Butler and John C. Walter, 131-147. New York: State University of New York Press, Albany, 1991.

Harris, Robert L., Jr., Darlene Clark Hine, and Nellie McKay. *Three Essays: Black Studies in the United States*. New York: The Ford Foundation, 1990.

Hatton, Ed. "The Future of Women's Studies: A Ford Foundation Workshop Report." *Women's Studies Quarterly* 22 (3 & 4) (Fall/Winter 1994): 256-264.

Hine, Darlene Clark. "Black Studies: An Overview." In *Three Essays: Black Studies in the United States*, edited by Robert L. Harris, Jr., Darlene Clark Hine, and Nellie McKay, 15-25. New York: The Ford Foundation, 1990.

Howe, Florence, and Mariam K. Chamberlain, eds. "Women's Studies: A World View." *Women's Studies Quarterly* 22 (3 & 4) (Fall/Winter 1994): 1-269.

Hull, Gloria T., Patricia Bell Scott, and Barbara Smith, eds. *All the Women Are White, All the Blacks Are Men, but Some of Us Are Brave: Black Women's Studies*. Old Westbury, NY: Feminist Press, 1982.

Levine, Arthur, ed. *Shaping Higher Education's Future: Demographic Realities and Opportunities, 1990-2000*. San Francisco: Jossey-Bass Publishers, 1989.

Levine, Arthur, and Jeannette Cureton. "The Quiet Revolution: Eleven Facts About Multiculturalism and the Curriculum." *Change* 24 (1) (January/February 1992): 25-29.

Luebke, Barbara F., and Mary E. Reilly. *Women's Studies Graduates: The First Generation*. New York: Teachers College Press, 1995.

McIntosh, Peggy. *Interactive Phases of Curricular Re-vision: A Feminist Perspective*. Working Papers Series, no. 124. Wellesley, MA: Center for Research on Women, 1983.

Miller, Connie, and Corinna Treitel. *Feminist Research Methods: An Annotated Bibliography*. New York: Greenwood Press, 1991.

Mingle, James R. *Black and Hispanic Enrollment in Higher Education, 1978: Trends in the Nation and South.* Atlanta, GA: Southern Regional Education Board, 1980.

Morris, Libby V. "Dependence in the Rural South." *Southern Journal of Rural Sociology* 10 (1) (1994): 115-130.

Musil, Caryn McTighe, ed. *The Courage to Question: Women's Studies and Student Learning.* Washington, DC: Association of American Colleges, 1992.

Musil, Caryn McTighe, and Ruby Sales. "Funding Women's Studies." In *Transforming the Curriculum: Ethnic Studies and Women's Studies,* edited by Johnnella E. Butler and John C. Walter, 21-34. New York: State University of New York Press, Albany, 1991.

O'Barr, Jean Fox. *Feminism in Action: Building Institutions and Community Through Women's Studies.* Chapel Hill, NC: The University of North Carolina Press, 1994.

National Women's Studies Association Task Force for the Association of American Colleges. *Liberal Learning and the Women's Studies Major.* Washington, DC: Association of American Colleges, 1991.

Schmitz, Betty. *Core Curriculum and Cultural Pluralism: A Guide for Campus Planners.* Washington, DC: Association of American Colleges, 1992.

Schuster, Marilyn R., and Susan R. VanDyne, eds. *Women's Place in the Academy.* Totowa, NJ: Rowman & Allanheld Publishers, 1985.

Wetzel, Jodi, and others, editors. *Women's Studies: Thinking Women.* Dubuque, IA: Kendall/Hunt Publishing Company, 1993.

Zinnser, Judith P. *History and Feminism: A Glass Half Full.* New York: Twayne Publishers, 1993.

# RATIONALE

The impact of multiculturalism on the academy has been pervasive, profound, and continuing. All segments — from two-year community colleges to the state four-year "flagships" to the Ivy elites — have felt, to some extent, the effects of what has become an ongoing, often contentious debate, whether manifested by tangible curricular changes; internecine disciplinary feuds; or controversial, sometimes divisive issues, such as speech codes and minority centers.

In some instances, whole new areas of study, such as African-American and women's studies have been added, sometimes at the expense of other, more traditional curricular components. At the same time, reform-minded scholars continue to advocate reappraisals of the criteria for choosing, for example, the authors included in — and by logical extension, those excluded from— literary studies or the perspectives through which historical phenomena are examined. One result of such significant shifts and controversies has been a proliferation of writing that examines the nature of the debates, the rationales underlying the various fundamental propositions, and the effects of all this on existing and potentially new curricular paradigms within the academy.

One significant factor affecting the expanding influence of the proponents of multiculturalism is the changing demographics of both faculties and student populations. Numerous writers have charted, for example, the growing number of women and minorities in higher education over the last fifteen years; these new constituents, quite simply, bring new sets of institutional demands. Frequently, writers describe and analyze the concomitant growth of power that these groups wield and the educational impact of such a shift. Numerous writers analyze, also, the continuing effects that movement and migration have had in this basic shift: for instance, the burgeoning growth in America of the Hispanic and Latino/Latina population and the large influx of Asian people, especially Southeast Asians since the fall of Saigon in 1975 and the serious refugee problems of Laos and Cambodia.

Another large body of literature discusses from the perspectives of both the traditional minorities and the traditional majority — usually construed as white males — these dynamic shifts in number and influence. Usually involved in such discussions are a range of issues seminal to higher education: for example, the specifics of integrating into the traditional curriculum material that reflects the experiences of those who feel newly enfranchised; the impact on pedagogy, methodology, and ways of learning implied by reformers; and the reactionary responses by traditionalists, both individuals, such as the late Allan Bloom of the University of Chicago, and groups, such as the National Association of Scholars. Specifically, the latter argue that multicultural reform brings curricular fragmentation and a dilution of academic standards.

On the other hand, many writers contend that multiculturalism is the wedge for opening higher education to a much needed breath of intellectual fresh air. They argue that opposition to thoughtful, reasoned change is smug, and contradictory to the notion of expansive academic freedom that is the superstructure of the academy. To these academicians, reform generated out of multicultural debate is simply the next step in the ongoing pursuit of knowledge and the ways to approach, analyze, and utilize that knowledge. Realistically, too, they argue, how is it intellectually justifiable or socially realistic for higher education largely to ignore the vast experiences of women — at least half of the population at any given time — and of the myriad of groups who compose our country? Plus, they continue, the world is "shrinking," and the need for more expansive and more inclusive perspectives is imperative at all levels of our national existence.

Writers in this vein, such as Johnnella Butler, Betty Schmitz, Marilyn Schuster, and Susan Van Dyne, analyze, for instance, the evolution of ethnic studies and women's studies and explore the institutional challenges to successful curricular transformation. This group of writers also debate such issues as the potential and the pitfalls in what would appear as natural linkages between women's studies and ethnic studies. Implied in much of this type of writing is the argument not only that traditional curricular models are inflexible and unacceptable, but also that new models should develop only through a careful, organic process of analysis that goes beyond the initial flush of victory over mere disciplinary existence: by asking, for instance, what are our guiding principles? where are there areas for philosophical and disciplinary alliances? how do we ameliorate the potential for our own disciplinary parochialism, an attribute that we have heartily criticized in traditional studies? Others, of course, join this debate at a number of levels, from the problematic need for serious curricular reexamination to the question of whether the engine that drives the multicultural agenda is political, not intellectual or academic.

Discussions of rationale often are clearly dichotomous. On the one hand, many of those who support the educational mandates of multiculturalism assert that American higher education is too slow to change, too imbued with the influence of the existing power structure and the weight of ingrained traditionalism. On the other hand, many supportive of that structure argue both for the academic and intellectual value that they see in the "traditional" — that which has stood the test of time and scrutiny — and for a recognition that the academy is, indeed, amenable to reasonable calls for change.

Numerous specifics are offered to substantiate the latter claim: for instance, the manner in which higher education assimilated the huge influx of post-World War II students; the rapidity with which science, math, and technology were expanded on the campus in the late 1950s after Russia's Sputnik; the birth and growth of the "multiversity" concept and of technical and community colleges; and the curricular responses to the outcry for "relevance" in the 1960s. The multiculturalists counter with the question of whether such changes mainly were externally imposed and unavoidable and, as a matter of fact, peripheral and token rather than fundamental and inclusive. Currently these issues are far from resolved.

Regardless, however, of whether writers emphasize tradition or reform, the intensity behind the various arguments implies that multiculturalism is a continuing force with which the academy must contend. And as even more historically marginalized groups — for example, Chicano/Chicana, Native Americans, those from the Pacific Rim, and gays and lesbians — gain power and the impetus to act, the debate will continue.

**Rationale**

1.  Adams, Maurianne, ed. *Promoting Diversity in College Classrooms: Innovative Responses for the Curriculum, Faculty, and Institutions*. New Directions for Teaching and Learning, no. 52. San Francisco: Jossey-Bass Publishers, 1992. 152 pp.

    Divides the essays into three parts: (1) new perspectives on teaching and learning (a faculty-development model for analysis and action, the understanding of classroom and campus racial dynamics, and the handling of bias issues in the classroom), (2) social diversity in the curriculum (an analysis of differences and commonalities between international and multicultural education, cultural pluralism and core curricula, diversity in required writing courses, and the design of a course that addresses both social diversity and social justice), and (3) social diversity on college campuses (the incorporation of social diversity at three public universities, Miami-Dade Community College and Joliet Junior College, institutional transformation for multicultural education at Bloomfield College and St. Norbert College).

2.  Andersen, Margaret L. "Changing the Curriculum in Higher Education." *Signs: Journal of Women in Culture and Society* 12 (2) (1987): 222-254.

    Overview of why and how to build a more inclusive curriculum. Includes a critique of the three most commonly used methods that curriculum-change projects use to describe this greater inclusion of women's scholarship: mainstreaming, integrating women's studies into the curriculum, and gender-balancing the curriculum. Lists a number of specific projects and then details the phases of curricular change, examines major changes that inclusive-curricular changes effect in a number of disciplines, and presents some fundamental resource materials.

3.  Auletta, Gales S., and Terry Jones, eds. "The Inclusive University: Multicultural Perspectives in Higher Education."

*American Behavioral Scientist* 34 (2) (November/December 1990): 133-278.

Divides this issue into three major categories: (1) *Redefining the University, Its Culture, and Its Research Methods* (articles on theory and the other, challenges across the curriculum, and promotion of multicultural dissertation research in a Eurocentric university), (2) *The Inclusive University: Making Cultural Diversity Happen* (articles on mentoring and cultural diversity in academic settings, debunking the myth of a monolithic white culture in America, science as both another and a part of culture, and the university president's role in realizing the multicultural university) and (3) *Dialect Diversity: How to Communicate and Share Knowledge in the Multicultural University* (articles on the primacy of standard language in modern education, public speaking instruction and cultural bias, the role of ebonics [black language] and ethnic studies in the university, and the need for a paradigm shift to recognize diversity).

4.  Bagasao, Paula Y., and Bob H. Suzuki, eds. "Asian and Pacific Americans: Behind the Myths." *Change* 21 (6) (November/December 1989): 12-63.

Includes articles on Asian Americans as the perceived *model minority*, the demographics of Asian Americans in higher education, Asian and Pacific students' discussions of their educational experiences, the Asian-American admissions debate (*a quota on excellence?*), empowerment of Asian-American faculty, the arts and the Asian-American community, and the role of Asian-American studies in U.S. higher education ("opening the American mind and body").

5.  Banks, James A. *An Introduction to Multicultural Education.* Boston: Allyn and Bacon, 1994. 136 pp.

Serves as a comprehensive resource to the many issues, concerns, and paradigms for multicultural education. Begins with a succinct overview of the aims of multicultural education, the debate over the canon, and the variety of approaches to multicultural education. Discusses the meaning and goals of multicultural education and the levels to a transformed curriculum. Gives the knowledge categories needed for becoming effective multicultural teachers, along with examples for teaching. Concludes with benchmarks for assessing progress toward a multicultural education. Provides in the references a guide to the many works in this area by the author.

6.    Bassey, Magnus O. "Multicultural Education: Its Unexplored Philosophical Themes." *The Western Journal of Black Studies* 17 (4) (1993): 202-208.

Describes the philosophical underpinnings of multicultural education as existentialism and humanistic/critical educational theory. Cites examples from Rogers, Sartre, Kirkegaard, Banks, W.E.B. Dubois, and others to illustrate the linkages between these theories. Asserts that multiculturalism is essentially the brainchild of Western academic tradition and ideals. Notes that the current multicultural education movement originated with black studies and the civil rights movement. Stresses the attention that multicultural education provides in addressing the individual and group issues of hopelessness, helplessness, oppression, and the ultimate goal of individual empowerment. Sees the aims of education in each perspective as serving individual needs and sharing the belief that every individual can, should, and must learn. Calls for active learning and education concerned with human existence in its cultural and historical context.

7.    Bloom, Allan. *The Closing of the American Mind*. New York: Simon and Schuster, 1987. 392 pp.

Subtitled *How Education Has Failed Democracy and Impoverished the Souls of Today's Students*. Details a perception of the university as moving from a bastion of intellectual freedom to an arena where society's problems (e.g., much of the multifaceted impact of multiculturalism) are meant to be solved. Divides his argument into three major parts: (1) the evolving nature of students, (2) the American style of nihilism (e.g., the German influence; the concepts of self, creativity, and culture; and prevailing values), and (3) the nature of the university itself (e.g., the relation between thought and civil society, the impact of the 1960s, the decomposition of the academy, and the status of the disciplines). Includes an extensive authorial introduction and a preface by Nobel laureate Saul Bellow. (Chapter 1)

8.    Bossman, David M. "Cross-Cultural Values for a Pluralistic Core Curriculum." *The Journal of Higher Education* 62 (6) (November/December 1991): 661-681.

Proposes that the cross-cultural methodologies of the social sciences can be especially helpful in examining and understanding the range of values implicit in a core curriculum. Argues for a comparative study of world cultures, economies, philosophies, and political systems, a study he sees as representing the basic elements for any pluralistic society. Devotes approximately first two-thirds of the article to a mostly abstract, philosophic delineation of the terms cross-cultural and multicultural and to an examination of how values are formed in a pluralistic society.

9.    Brandon-Falcone, Janice, and others. "Teaching Cultural Diversity in the Core Curriculum." *The Journal of General Education* 43 (3) (1994): 230-240.

Notes that debates of multiculturalism often divide into two simplistic camps pitting the non-Western cultures against the Western world view. Advances that faculty at the undergraduate level must begin with students and develop the idea that diversity is not limited to ethnic, gender, and geographical diversity, but that pluralism also exists within societies. Gives examples of specific assignments used in teaching cultural diversity in literature, history, humanities, and philosophy. Concludes with the importance of including multiculturalism in the core of undergraduate studies to reach a large number of students while recognizing the importance of specific courses to address in depth issues of gender, race/ethnicity, and diversity.

10.    Bruno-Jofre, Rosa del Carmen, and Laura Lee Vance, eds. *Women in Higher Education: A Cross-Cultural Approach.* Western Washington University: Woodring College of Education, 1991. 216 pp.

Presents the proceedings of the conference *Women in Higher Education: A Multicultural Approach* at Western Washington University, April 12-22, 1989. Offers a thematic arrangement of the presentations in eight parts: (1) moving toward equality; (2) a look at student realities; (3) staff, faculty, and administrative issues; (4) retention of minorities and women (e.g., American Indian women in higher education); (5) developing an inclusive curriculum (e.g., how administrators can help and a view of the history curriculum at Western Washington University); (6) the search for a common ground (e.g., reclaiming the voice of minority women and analyzing intergenerational learning); (7) the question of personhood; and (8) the grassroots' voice in the change process (presents conference recommendations).

11.    Bryden, David P. "It Ain't What They Teach, It's The Way That They Teach It." *The Public Interest* 103 (Spring 1991): 38-53.

Defends the traditional canons against a concept of multiculturalism that he sees permeated by a penchant to have underlying egalitarian creeds that are dogmatic and fallacious and a political rather than curricular agenda. Relates multicultural curricula to affirmative action and to the liberal left's nurturing of campus radicalism. Surmises that, in the final analysis, the struggle within universities should continue but that there should be a clear realization of what this struggle truly involves: not what curricular content should be, per se, but rather, how it should be taught.

12. Butler, Johnnella E. "The Difficult Dialogue of Curriculum Transformation: Ethnic Studies and Women's Studies." In *Transforming the Curriculum: Ethnic Studies and Women's Studies*, edited by Johnnella E. Butler and John C. Walter, 1-19. Albany, NY: State University of New York Press, 1991.

Examines some of the traditional critics who generally oppose curricular change initiated by what they see as the growing politicization of multicultural proponents. Decries the tendency to reform the curriculum simply by adding here and there a course on women's studies or ethnic studies. Presents as the necessary and logical alternative a paradigm for radically transforming these two fundamental areas: women's studies must be less white and ideologically feminist (primacy of gender) and ethnic studies must be less male-centered. Presents seven of the academy's basic ills and offers suggestions for specific changes, using English literature as an example.

13. Butler, Johnnella, and Betty Schmitz. "Ethnic Studies, Women's Studies, and Multiculturalism." *Change* 24 (1) (January/February 1992): 37-41.

Discusses how ethnic women's studies evolved and some of the impacts they have had on higher education. Also examines how their purposes often have been misconstrued and what the authors perceive as problems in the discipline becoming a leader in multicultural initiatives. Addresses some of the major critics of multicultural curricular transformation and reviews a sample of 102 preprogram and postprogram syllabi from 6 disciplines on 33 campuses. Explores some of the institutional challenges to successful curricular change.

14. Chace, William M. "The Real Challenge of Multiculturalism (Is Yet to Come)." *Academe* 76 (6) (November/December 1990): 20-23.

Outlines philosophically and pragmatically the strengths and weaknesses of what multiculturalism can become.

Distinguishes between the (1) formally academic (canon revision, inclusion of both high and popular culture, and inclusion of new genres of expression from around the world) and the (2) political (race, ethnicity, gender, sexual preference, and power acquisition inside the academy) components of the term multiculturalism. Describes the kinds of curricula that these two distinct camps would probably advocate. Also explores the need to move beyond the friction and debates engendered by these rather competitive and volatile components, to find areas of mutuality in what is apparently dissimilar, and to de-emphasize aspects of each that are specialized and formalized.

15.    Cheatham, Harold E., and others. *Cultural Pluralism on Campus*. Alexandria, VA: American Association for Counseling and Development, 1991. 205 pp.

Presents a student-affairs perspective on the academy's response to racial and social diversity. Divides the chapters/essays into three parts: (1) the resolution of inequality (affirming affirmative action and developing identity in a pluralistic society), (2) developmental needs (the minority cultural center on a predominately white campus, organization and administrative implications for serving students with disabilities, the role of developmental education in promoting pluralism, the integration of diversity into traditional resident-assistant courses, the planning of programs for cultural pluralism, National Collegiate Athletic Association policies and the African-American student athlete, and campus racial violence), and (3) funding and evaluating cultural pluralism programming (a case study of a large, eastern, public university and the evaluation of university programming for ethnic minority students).

16.    Cheney, Lynne V. "Multiculturalism Done Right: Taking Steps to Build Support for Change." *Change* 25 (1) (January/February 1993): 8-10.

Acknowledges that America is a multicultural society and this fact should be taught in all schools, colleges, and universities. Argues, however, that significant resistance to multiculturalism will be met unless certain fundamental principles underlie our teaching efforts. Presents and discusses the three principles that she feels are paramount in underpinning our efforts: We must (1) tell the complete truth while eschewing the revisionist myth or half-truth and the tendency to turn education into therapy; (2) remember to balance the new with the traditional, thus ensuring that multiculturalism offers more for everyone rather than less for anyone; and (3) emphasize what is common, what we share, as well as that which makes us unique.

17.  Cornwell, Grant H., and Eve W. Stoddard. "Things Fall Together: A Critique of Multicultural Curricular Reform." *Liberal Education* 80 (4) (Fall 1994): 40-51.

Describes the problems with multiculturalism and diversity as perspectives in general education and proceeds to describe the advantages of *intercultural* studies. Advances that multiculturalism and diversity alone do not adequately consider common needs across cultures. Describes the division between those who work on issues of American cultural pluralism and those working on global cultural encounter. Discusses problems with international education (e.g., makes the nation the object of study and tends to obscure diversity issues within countries) and notes the shift toward global studies that consider complex commonalities and differences both across and within cultures. Calls for intercultural study that is interdisciplinary and avoids the territoriality and isolated analysis characteristic of disciplines. Examines the question of *who* can speak to ethnic, racial, and cultural issues. Concludes with the goals of intercultural general education.

18.  Diner, Hasia R. "Some Problems with 'Multiculturalism'; or, 'The Best Laid Plans . . . '." *American Quarterly* 45 (2) (June 1993): 301-308.

Acknowledges the pervasiveness of references to multiculturalism but points out a number of disturbing characteristics of the movement, beginning with its multiple implications. Notes, also, that teaching and writing about those considered outside the mainstream have been increasingly incorporated into both secondary and higher-education curricula since the 1960's. Calls into question and analyzes the notion that the study of American culture as a history of multiple experiences is new and revolutionary. At the same time, discusses the existence and necessity of seeing a core of cultural values. Presents cautionary remarks about how contemporary multiculturalism can improve curricula or campus climate, especially in the classroom. Presents the argument that, ironically, multiculturalism may be close to being racist and sexist by the inherent nature of lumping individuals into disparate categories. Argues, finally, for a reasonable balance between unyielding traditionalism and suspect multiculturalism.

19.    DuBois, Ellen Carol, and others. *Feminist Scholarship: Kindling in the Groves of Academe*. Urbana, IL: University of Illinois Press, 1985. 227 pp.

Presents the subject of the development of feminist scholarship within and outside the academic disciplines. Includes three divisions: (1) the perspective from the disciplines (i.e., feminism arises in the disciplines), (2) feminist questions as guides for research (e.g., women's oppression, liberation, equality), and (3) the response of the disciplines from ten years of feminist scholarship. Includes an index and a selected bibliography.

20.    Dudovitz, Resa L., ed. *Women in Academe*. Elmsford, NY: Pergamon Press, Inc., 1984. 131-244 pp.

Along with a progress report on affirmative action, includes an editorial and three other parts: (1) the personal as political (black women faculty/white university), (2) feminist strategies in the academy (e.g., the role of graduate teaching assistants in effecting curriculum change, feminist collaboration and research strategies), and (3) women as the *other* academics (interaction of men and women's careers in academe and a discussion of women's work in sociology).

21. Edwards, Ronald G. "Multiculturalism and Its Link to Quality Education and Democracy." *Multicultural Review* 2 (2) (June 1993): 12-14.

Traces the concept of multiculturalism to the 1920s and the terms — *intercultural, multiethnic,* and *intergroup* — used in earlier decades. Connects the recent resurgence in multiculturalism to the civil rights movement and changes in the immigration patterns, beginning in the 1960s, that bring more Third World people to the United States. Notes the lack of a clear definition of multiculturalism and the confusion introduced by placing global or international education under this broad concept. Distinguishes between the pluralists' and particularists' beliefs in a common culture: the former are optimistic and the latter are not. Concludes with a call for educators to show leadership in providing instruction about diverse cultures and values without falling prey to various extremes.

22. Farrant, Patricia A., and Alice Miller, eds. "Women's Centers." *Initiatives* 51 (2 & 3) (Summer 1988): 3-53.

Presents articles that examine the origins and underlying philosophy of women's centers and their organizational structures, programmatic strategies, and problems. Includes articles that profile these campus centers, analyze their frameworks, and examine them from a number of perspectives: the center as *the new dean of women,* the diversity and success of The University of Iowa Women's Resource and Action Center, multicultural programming in a university women's center, the revitalization of a campus center, career centers· as women's centers, and women's centers and women administrators.

23.    Feinberg, Walter. *Japan and the Pursuit of a New American Identity: Work and Education in Multicultural Age.* New York: Routledge, 1993. 216 pp.

Examines the prescriptive argument that America can decrease many of its educational and economic ills by emulating much of the Japanese model. Argues that American education is constrained by a philosophy that casts students and schools as weapons in global competition with the Japanese. Suggests a vision of education that supports the growing cultural diversity of American society and educational institutions. Interviews and analyzes American and Japanese workers, managers, parents, and teachers. Argues that our schools can engage the formation of a new multicultural America and chart a course for reform in education.

24.    Gaudiani, Claire. "In Pursuit of Global Civic Virtues." *Liberal Education* 77 (3) (May/June 1991): 12-15.

States that those who desire a greater multicultural orientation in the curriculum must share explicitly the rationale for such a change. Defends multiculturalism and a broad, culturally diverse curriculum as the most logical methods of developing modern civic virtues. Using the notion of an increasingly interdependent world, develops the idea that a multicultural curriculum is the only really feasible way by which those who would advance democratic values can analyze the virtues that can make this world more livable for all. Also, discusses communal responsibilities, the need to search for common ground, and the need to lessen the pernicious impact of ethnocentric particularism and racial or ethnic stereotyping.

25.    Ginorio, Angela B., and others, eds. "Curricular and Institutional Change." *Women's Studies Quarterly* 18 (1 & 2) (Spring/Summer 1990): 231.

Divides change into three categories — curriculum transformation, pedagogy, and institutional change — and includes articles on the design of an inclusive core curriculum; the Ford Foundation Program on *Mainstreaming Minority Women's Study*; a case for an academic minor in women of color; a method for starting a program in Chicana studies; the *Gender Integration Project* at Piscataway Township School; women's studies from an international perspective; the barriers to curricular restructuring; the American Anthropological Association Project on *Gender and the Curriculum*; the integration of gender, race, and ethnicity into experimental psychology and other social-science methodology courses; the fostering of positive race, class, and gender dynamics; the dynamics of a global classroom; a women's studies course exploring privilege and racism; the implications for faculty of Supreme Court decisions on sex discrimination; a case study on the feminist transformation of a university; the *Minnesota Plan II* for improving the university environment for women faculty, administrators, and academic professional staff; an investigation of sexual-harassment complaints; and the evolution of an inclusive language policy at Emory & Henry College.

26.   Goddard, Nancy T., and others, eds. "The Curriculum Integration Movement: Taking a Closer Look." *Women's Studies Quarterly* 13 (2) (Summer 1985): 15-25.

Includes articles on the incorporation of perspectives on women into the curriculum (a Ford Foundation workshop), reports on curriculum-integration projects, the standard forms of information organization (academic libraries and curriculum integration), and recent books on curriculum integration. Also examines (1) the ways in which new research on women affects the natural sciences and (2) the development of a course on women in international development.

27.   Goldstein, Barry. "Cultural Diversity and Curricular Coherence." In *Changing College Classrooms: New Teaching and Learning Strategies for an Increasingly Complex World*, edited by Diane F. Halpern and associates, 109-127. San Francisco: Jossey-Bass Publishers, 1994.

Presents an overview of the need for multicultural education in colleges and universities, noting changing student profiles, new knowledge, equality, and market demands. Acknowledges more widespread involvement of the social sciences and literature in multicultural education, but emphasizes that even the *hard sciences* are rich fields for multicultural teaching and learning. Gives, as an example for a more inclusive curriculum, brief descriptions of content areas that could be used to illustrate coherence and diversity in biology.

28.    Goodstein, Lynne. "Achieving a Multicultural Curriculum: Conceptual, Pedagogical, and Structural Issues." *The Journal of General Education* 43 (2) (1994): 102-116.

Reviews the two dominant methods for multicultural change in undergraduate curricula: (1) curriculum transformation projects and (2) revised general education requirements. Advances that diversity must be defined and operationalized using either method and then examines the concept of diversity as a critical perspective and diversity defined as variety. Describes four structural conditions that may affect implementation of multicultural courses and perspectives: (1) financial, (2) organizational resistance to change, (3) political opposition, and (4) coalitions. Concludes that the model of diversity as variety is more likely to thrive in higher education.

29.    Henry, Charles P., and Frances Smith Foster. "Black Women's Studies: Threat or Challenge?" *The Western Journal of Black Studies* 6 (1) (1982): 15-21.

Analyzes some of the early problems that confronted black women's studies. Focuses primarily on (1) the preponderance of white women who then held most positions of power and influence within the discipline and (2) the male bias of those who were instrumental in the early black nationalist movement, thus imbuing black studies overall with a lack of incentives for black female advancement. Also includes a historical perspective, an identification of some misconceptions about black women's studies, and suggestions for growth and comprehensive improvement.

30. Higginbotham, Elizabeth. "Designing an Inclusive Curriculum: Bringing All Women into the Core." *Women's Studies Quarterly* 18 (1 & 2) (Spring/Summer 1990): 7-23.

Discusses what is seen as the three most important tasks necessary for a successful curricular transformation: (1) gain information about the diversity of the female experience, (2) decide how this new material is to be taught, and (3) ensure that all students feel comfortable in the classroom environment. Gives a critique of the traditional curriculum, especially in relation to the treatment of people of color. Emphasizes and defends the need for a major overhaul of the curriculum, not just the appending of a few courses onto the present structure. Details the need for faculty development and an interdisciplinary approach, both predicated on a movement away from marginalization caused by the prevailing white, middle-class, heterosexual American norm.

31. Hilgers, Thomas, Marie Wunsch, and Virgie Chattergy, eds. *Academic Literacies in Multicultural Higher Education: Selected Essays.* Manoa, HI: Center for Studies of Multicultural Higher Education, University of Hawaii at Manoa, 1992. 189 pp.

Divides the essays into three divisions: (1) perspectives on literacy and academic culture (e.g., culture and academic literacy, liberal education in a multicultural democracy, and multiple literacies and the reading of literature), (2) issues and research related to multiculturalism in higher education (e.g., the concept of gender reflection in writing, interdisciplinary team teaching in a culturally diverse educational context, the behavior dynamics assessment model as a tool for multicultural higher education, learning among ethnically diverse nursing students and faculty, and error patterns in research papers by Pacific Rim students), and (3) changing classrooms and programs (e.g., strategies for antihomophobic pedagogy, using journals to teach multicultural students on interactive television, tensions and ironies in multicultural textbooks, demystifying writing across disciplinary and cultural bounds, and enriching the climate for diversity through faculty development).

32.    Hill, Patrick J. "Multi-Culturalism: The Crucial Philosophical and Organizational Issues." *Change* 23 (4) (July/August 1991): 38-47.

Discusses the underlying philosophical and organizational issues in the current debate about multiculturalism. Explores the nature of the concept of diversity, especially in the context of Western philosophical development from Montaigne and Descartes forward. Examines the ethical imperative of linking diverse opinions in political and epistemological, as well as philosophical, traditions. Extols the virtues of democratic pluralism, a framework for understanding diversity that welcomes, respects, fosters, and even celebrates the inherent differentness of the world yet searches for, and logically accommodates, any commonalities. Calls for and describes a higher education community and curriculum that are both interdisciplinary and intercultural rather than just multicultural. Examines possible objections to his paradigm.

33.    Jayne, Edward. "Academic Jeremiad: The Neoconservative View of American Higher Education." *Change* 23 (3) (May/June 1991): 30-41.

Dissects some of the major critics (e.g., Bloom, Sykes, Shaw, Kimball, Bromwich, and Short) of multiculturalism. Asserts that as academic neoconservatives, these authors seem dedicated to the assumption that the multicultural movement is dramatically weakening American education and that professors must come to the defense of traditional scholarly values. Notes, however, that many differences still exist among these critics, and, therefore, a monolithic lumping together of their ideas and criticisms does little good to anyone seriously interested in higher education improvement. Distills what he sees as useful from their arguments and asserts the need for balance, a search for some middle ground between them and the multiculturalists.

34. Jules-Rosette, Bennetta. "The Dual Vision: Insights and Applications of Cross-Cultural Research." *Journal of Negro Education* 55 (2) (1986): 125-141.

   Critiques the American anthropological tendency — promulgated mainly during and immediately after the 1930s — to emphasize the homogeneity of world views, which he feels are commonly held beliefs and attitudes about the way the world operates. Argues that such an emphasis is overly simple and reductionist, especially the tendency to view cultures as internally similar; this tends to de-emphasize multicultural experiences and fails to give proper weight to cultural change and conflict. Discusses the need for intercultural exchange and the ability to see both single cultures and, at the same time, a synthesized world view. Applies this refined anthropological notion to multicultural education.

35. Kalantzis, Mary, and William Cope. "Multiculturalism May Prove to be the Key Issue of Our Epoch." *The Chronicle of Higher Education* 39 (11) (November 4, 1992): B3, B5.

   Stresses the transrational nature and importance of dealing with cultural diversity. Stresses, also, the need for scholarly patience in incorporating new multicultural components into the curriculum: for example, the need to view innovative courses on racial or ethnic groups with a broader understanding of their intellectual role and potential and to recognize that in any intellectual innovation in academe, new paradigms and theories need both time and space for incorporation. Proposes that higher education redefine studies by shedding a parochial view and becoming more aware of the international basis of contemporary living and learning.

36.     Kessler-Harris, Alice. "The View from Women's Studies."
        *Signs: The Journal of Women in Culture and Society* 17 (4)
        (Summer 1992): 794-804.

        Analyzes one of the most serious, ongoing problems for
        women's studies: bearing the responsibility for supporting
        the growth of multiculturalism while attempting to resolve
        internal issues of political correctness. Describes the dual
        problems of being singled out as one of the specific areas that
        erode traditional academic values on the one hand, and, on
        the other hand, fighting against those internal forces that
        hinder the growth of women as individuals or as under
        represented group members. Examines the strengths and
        weaknesses of her own program at Rutgers University and
        extrapolates from these to those of women's studies in
        general. Argues for acknowledgement and discussion of
        internal differences and dissensions as the best means for
        problem resolution and disciplinary coherence and
        advancement.

37.     Kimball, Roger. *Tenured Radicals: How Politics Has Corrupted
        Our Higher Education.*    New York: Harper and Row
        Publishers, Inc., 1990. 204 pp.

        Explores what the author perceives as ideologically
        motivated assaults on the academy, as well as on our culture.
        Includes chapters dealing with the assault on the canon, a
        critique of the 1989 report Speaking for the Humanities and
        the journal *October* (both defenders of the new critics of
        traditional academic practice), a critical profile of Paul
        deMan, the emergence and dynamics of deconstruction, the
        language and logic of the liberal criticism (especially Stanley
        Fish, head of the Department of English, Duke University),
        and the author's perception of the real crisis in the
        humanities. Also includes a selected bibliography.

38.     King, William M. "Challenges Across the Curriculum:
        Broadening the Bases of How Knowledge is Produced."
        *American Behavioral Scientist* 34 (2) (November/December
        1990): 165-180.

Recommends and defends the need to have a greater Afrocentric orientation in understanding and teaching the social sciences. Discusses limitations of the traditional Eurocentric research orientation, especially the underlying cultural bias in social science's use of scientific methods and its tendency for research results simply to justify previously held beliefs, even in the most subjectively constructed methodology. Describes the Afrocentric orientation — synthetic and transdisciplinary — and shows how this can be applied to effect positive change in higher-education curricula.

39.   La Fromboise, Teresa D., and Barbara S. Plake. "Toward Meeting the Research Needs of American Indians." *Harvard Educational Review* 53 (1) (February 1983): 45-51.

Discusses what the authors see as a culturally myopic view that characterizes most of the research done on the heritage and social behavior of American Indians. Analyzes the cultural and academic impediments that tend to leave Indians themselves severely underrepresented in doctoral and graduate programs in education and, thus, in their own cultural research. Presents strategies for including more American Indians in higher-education programs that could lead to greater participation in research: for example, establishment of research institutes at selected universities, expanded internships, and mentor/fellow investigative relationships. Presents a prescriptive discussion of how to integrate into higher education a multicultural curriculum that more closely serves Indian purposes.

40.   Levine, Arthur, ed. "The Curriculum and Multiculturalism." *Change* 24 (1) (January/February 1992): 12-73.

Includes articles on political correctness and the press; the curriculum *crusades* and the conservative backlash; eleven facts about multiculturalism and the curriculum; the educational issues inherent in multicultural education; ethnic studies, women's studies, and multiculturalism; continuity and change in literature study; practical lessons (i.e., what not to do); engaging faculty in the issue; and three major questions for the multiculturalism debate.

41.    Mattai, P. Rudy. "Rethinking the Nature of Multicultural Education: Has it Lost its Focus or is it Being Misused?" *Journal of Negro Education* 61 (1) (1992): 65-77.

Assesses the state of multicultural studies overall and their failure to address adequately the problems that necessitate their existence. Focuses on the paradoxical inability of multicultural education to address the issue of race and on the lack of institutional commitment to the present curricular configuration. Analyzes the basic definitional problems of multicultural education and explores its failure to enfranchise educationally those who should most logically reap the rewards of such curricular expansion. Explores some of the problems inherent in injecting race into the higher education curriculum. Offers some prescriptive suggestions and an extensive bibliography.

42.    McCarthy, Cameron, ed. *Race and Curriculum: Social Inequality and the Theories and Politics of Difference in Contemporary Research on Schooling*. New York: The Falmer Press, 1990. 158 pp.

Strives to put into a theoretical and political perspective the issues of racial inequality and minority underachievement in schools and universities nationwide. Includes chapters on race and curriculum, mainstream accounts of racial inequality in schooling, the *multicultural solution*, neo-Marxist approaches to inequality, social difference as an alternative perspective on race and schooling, and racial inequality and educational reform.

43.    Mechling, Jay. "Theory and the Other; or, Is This Session the Text?" *American Behavioral Scientist* 34 (2) (November/December 1990): 153-164.

Presents some general guidelines for a multicultural dialogue to effect curricular and pedagogical changes drawn from a conference entitled *From the Eurocentric University to the Multicultural University*. Begins with a discussion of the propositions that define, generally, the concept of culture and, specifically, the concept of American culture. Assesses the curricular and pedagogical implications of these propositions and offers some specific suggestions for institutional consideration. Includes a look at two areas, faculty development/participation and the possibility of an appropriate course during freshman orientation, that she feels deserve greater consideration.

44.    Miller, Margaret A., and Anne-Marie McCartan. "At the Crossings: Making the Case for New Interdisciplinary Programs." *Change* 22 (3) (May/June 1990): 28-35.

Discusses reasons for the growing popularity of interdisciplinary programs, including their ability to (1) initiate new programs without unnecessary duplication; (2) allow an institution to begin high-quality programs in a small, new field rather than a lesser-quality one in an established field; and (3) attract students and stimulate faculty in a new way. Offers a number of specific questions to ask and guidelines to use in the all-important task of generating criteria for program evaluation. Includes generous discussions concerning quality issues, funding, organization, level of student interest, and the job market for graduates.

45.    Minnich, Elizabeth, Jean O'Barr, and Rachel Rosenfeld, eds. *Reconstructing the Academy: Women's Education and Women's Studies*. Chicago: The University of Chicago Press, 1988. 312 pp.

Presents essays originally appearing in various issues of *Signs: Journal of Women in Culture and Society*. Includes the education of women as philosophers, university definitions of sexual harassment, changing the curriculum in higher education, the theory and practice of women's studies, resistance to curriculum integration, overcoming internalized oppression and domination, the education of women in America, women's colleges and women achievers, the search for women role models, and the identity crisis in feminist theory (i.e., *cultural feminism versus poststructuralism*). Also includes a list of related interest articles from *Signs*.

46.    National Association of Scholars. "Is the Curriculum Biased? A Statement by the National Association of Scholars." *The Chronicle of Higher Education* 36 (10) (November 8, 1989): A23.

States (in a full-page advertisement) the central positions of an association that is now characterized as one of the most vocal proponents of maintaining higher education's traditional curricular values and orientation. Presents the six general justifications offered by those favoring a greater multicultural curriculum and then disputes the first five and argues that the sixth entails something other than the changes being proposed. Solicits the approval and backing of like-minded colleagues and gives an address and phone number for the receipt of further information.

47.    Nicholas, Ralph W. "Cultures in the Curriculum." *Liberal Education* 77 (3) (May/June 1991): 16-21.

From perspective of both dean and anthropologist, calls for discussions on culture and curriculum to return to some anthropological fundamentals. Acknowledges the significant differences among cultures but defends the larger notion of a culture of commonality that operates on the core assumption that, comparatively at least, Americans have vastly more in common with one another than any of them have with people who compose a cohort of, for example, racial, ethnic, or religious equals. Argues that we can all maintain the integrity of our individual values while accepting our common societal culture. Analyzes the unappealing nature of ethnocentrism and calls for the inculcation of a more thoughtful appreciation of our diversity.

48. O'Barr, Jean F., ed. "Reconstructing the Academy." *Signs: Journal of Women in Culture and Society* 12 (2) (Winter 1987): 203-385.

    Includes articles on the education of women as philosophers, curricular change in higher education, resistance to curriculum integration, the awkward relationship between feminism and anthropology, a Marxist perspective on curricular change, the history and philosophy of women in science, the education of women in America, and a female student in late-medieval Krakow.

49. Rodrigues, Raymond J. "Rethinking the Cultures of Disciplines." *The Chronicle of Higher Education* 38 (33) (April 29, 1992): B1-B2.

    Comments on the necessity of seeing the link between disciplinary diversity and cultural diversity. Postulates that strategies that work in conducting academic business related to the former can be used to inform and expand the latter. Discusses, first, the failure of academics to recognize that multicultural tensions can be found not only in matters of ethnicity and race, but also between and among disciplines. Thus, argues that the more that faculty members from diverse disciplines are brought together to solve common intellectual problems, the more they will begin to appreciate how the cultures of other disciplines influence their colleagues' thinking. Extrapolates from this healthy recognition of disciplinary diversity to the larger concept of cultural diversity.

50. Rude, Renee, and Robert Hauptman. "Multicultural Innovations: Curricular Reform in the Academy." *Multicultural Review* 1 (3) (July 1992): 18-19.

    Proposes a thoughtful, consistent approach to curricular revision: first, acknowledging and accepting past omissions and then, second, thoroughly examining the new mixture before actually restructuring the curriculum. Examines four ways by which ethnic content can be integrated into the classroom. Affirms the need to go beyond the defensive posture adapted by some of the most vocal traditionalists and to embrace the vitality and breadth of perspective that a multiculturalist approach can add to earlier curricula.

51.     Schmitz, Betty. "Diversity & Collegiality in the Academy." *Liberal Education* 77 (4) (September/October 1991): 19-22.

Notes the enormous changes (e.g., new populations of students and faculty and women's and ethnic studies) under way in higher education and assesses some of the resultant impacts. Presents a short background on resistance to these changes and then analyzes — and offers refutations of — three of the most prevalent claims of those resisting change: (1) this is a minority victims' revolution, (2) the choice is between retaining or abandoning Western civilization (the choice between retaining or compromising academic standards), (3) proponents of change try to enforce correct ways of thinking about race and gender. Acknowledges the excesses on both sides of this volatile issue and comments on the positive implications that true curricular transformation holds.

52.     Schmitz, Betty. *Core Curriculum and Cultural Pluralism: A Guide for Campus Planners*. Washington, DC: Association of American Colleges, 1992. 127 pp.

A guidebook based on an Association of American Colleges' project, Engaging Cultural Legacies: Shaping Core Curricula in the Humanities, funded by the National Endowment for the Humanities. Addresses the dual need for a core curriculum and the inclusion of cultural complexity and multiplicity as important themes in undergraduate education. Addresses challenges to content, pedagogy, and institutional structure. Shares key findings and emerging models for curricular transformation based on the experiences of 63 participating institutions. Discusses implementing and maintaining programs and provides a summary of features of strong programs. Includes a brief annotated bibliography.

53. Schuster, Marilyn R., and Susan R. Van Dyne, eds. *Women's Place in the Academy: Transforming the Liberal Arts Curriculum.* Totowa, NJ: Rowman & Allanheld, Publishers, 1985. 328 pp.

   Divides the chapters into four parts: (1) curriculum transformation (women as a catalyst for twenty-first century change, stages of curriculum transformation, a reassessment of coeducation, a redefinition of women's education, the necessity of a close alliance between women's and black studies, and the complications involved in a women's- and black-studies alliance), and (2) faculty development (a look at the Smith College model that combines faculty development with curricular change; a prescription for initiating a curriculum-integration project; a description of the national Summer Institute in Women's Studies, the Great Lakes Colleges Association; and resources shared at the Wheaton College Dissemination Conference), (3) classroom outcomes (*deconstructing* women's studies to *reconstructing* the humanities, rethinking philosophy, the transformation of a course in American literary realism, forms of resistance in communicating difference, a transformation of the social sciences, and the integration of the feminist perspective into courses in introductory biology), and (4) resources (including syllabus redesign guidelines and selected bibliography).

54. Schuster, Marilyn R., and Susan R. Van Dyne. "Placing Women in the Liberal Arts: Stages of Curriculum Transformation." *Harvard Educational Review* 54 (4) (November 1984): 413-428.

   Presents a paradigm that describes how teachers and students experience the process of curricular change. Explores the background of how scholarship on women has helped to redefine the core curriculum, especially as a force in initiating greater awareness of and an emphasis on multicultural and interdisciplinary perspectives. Argues that understanding women's experience in every culture is vitally important to every liberal arts course. Explores sources of institutional resistance and offers an analysis of their concept of the six stages of change that must occur for a true transformed, balanced curriculum. Proposes some of the characteristics of a transformed curriculum: for example, self-conscious methodology; changed content in a changed context; and meaningful attention to intersections of race, class, and cultural differences within gender.

55.    Sizemore, Barbara A. "The Politics of Curriculum, Race, and Class." *Journal of Negro Education* 59 (1) (1990): 77-85.

Defends the need for a greater multicultural perspective in higher education by exploring, in general, both the politics of curricular inclusion and exclusion and the very nature of culture and its relationship to education. Argues against the basis of the traditionalists' argument that Western European culture should be regarded as the national culture of the United States. Argues for a complete democratization of the national cultural ethos and, thus, the curricular inclusion of those categories marginalized by the traditional Eurocentric bias.

56.    Smith, Daryl G. "Embracing Diversity as a Central Campus Goal." *Academe* 76 (6) (November/December 1990): 29-33.

Suggests that truly multicultural campuses can exist only if the current framework is shifted "from one that focuses solely on assisting or accommodating those who are different so they can survive in an alien world, to creating a campus world that is not alien and that promotes success." Refutes the perception that increasing diversity must, necessarily, decrease quality, whether of students' abilities or curricular content. Explores the ways in which the disciplines are — and should — change and discusses the movement from early notions of a diverse community that assumed an assimilation model to a more contemporary one based on mutual respect and a celebration of differences. Describes some of the fundamental rethinking that must precede true curricular transformation.

57.    Stage, Frances K., and Kathleen Manning. *Enhancing the Multicultural Campus Environment: A Cultural Brokering*

*Approach.* New Directions for Student Services, number 60. San Francisco: Jossey-Bass Publishers, Winter 1992. 92 pp.

Includes chapters on the multicultural campus, the cultural-broker model for student-affairs educators, the administrative role in a diverse environment, academic concerns in a diverse environment, multicultural implications for students, the cultural broker in the living environment, the cultural broker and the cocurriculum, and a vision of the multicultural campus. Also includes three pages of annotated bibliography.

58.  Stone, Robert L. *Essays on 'The Closing of the American Mind'.* Chicago: Chicago Review Press, Inc., 1989. 382 pp.

Presents a comprehensive collection of essays divided into eleven sections: (1) a discussion that attempts to transcend the usual labels of *left* and *right* (e.g., a look at the liberals' defense of the canons and at criticism and praise), (2) the book's ascent to best-seller status (e.g., book reviews and analyses of its surprising mass appeal), (3) personal comments on Bloom the person and professor, (4) conflicting views on Bloom as an elitist, (5) conflicting views of Bloom's philosophical stance, (6) analyses of Bloom as an antifeminist (e.g., by Bloom himself and by Betty Friedan and Martha Nussbaum), (7) perspectives on Bloom's views of minority groups in the academy and of affirmative action, (8) his views on rock music, (9) the question of oversimplification and exaggeration in the book (e.g., the lack of alternatives for universities), (10) an assessment of Bloom's comments on the place of religion in his paradigm, and (11) the proper role of the university in a democratic society. Presents a total of 62 diverse essays.

59.  Thelin, John R. "The Curriculum Crusades and the Conservative Backlash." *Change* 24 (1) (January/February 1992): 17-23.

Analyzes the orthodoxies and organizations of the neoconservative view in the multiculturalism/political correctness debate in higher-education curricular matters. Postulates that American higher education lacks, rather than a middle ground, an academic common ground, an idea that runs somewhat counter to the general neoconservative call for a restoration within the curriculum of some previous state of harmony, tradition and shared values, perceived as a dubious statement of historical fact. Critiques, in particular, the works and statements of Dinesh D'Souza, author of *Illiberal Education*, and, more extensively, his ideological predecessor, Edward Shils, author of *The Academic Ethic*. Also looks at the 1990 controversy over a revision in the freshman writing course at the University of Texas. Assesses both the logic and coherence of the neoconservative faction and proposes that both sides in the often polarizing argument be brought together to search for that common ground.

60.   Walzer, Judith B. "New Knowledge or a New Discipline?: Women's Studies at the University." *Change* 14 (3) (April 1982): 21-23.

Discusses the development of women's studies, especially as an academic, rather than political, enterprise. Explores, specifically, the question of whether these studies should be considered a new discipline, thus implying the need for organization into separate departments within the curriculum, or a new subject matter, implying the gradual integration of new material into the existing curriculum. Argues the need for the establishment of a rigorous academic, intellectual base and the development, at least initially, of separate disciplinary entities and, simultaneously, the integration into the larger, more-established departments.

61.   Warehine, Nancy. *To Be One of Us: Cultural Conflict, Creative Democracy, and Education.* Albany: State University of New York Press, 1993. 190 pp.

Presents an analysis of writers, such as Allan Bloom, Cornel West, and William Bennett. Specifically, divides the examination into an introduction and six chapters: three views of the crises in humanities education and liberal democracy; the conservative discourse of crisis in the 1980s; responses to Allan Bloom's discourse of crisis (e.g., Martha Nussbaum, Richard Rorty, and Stanley Aronowitz); the impact of pragmatism on the crisis of the humanities; responses to Richard Rorty's liberal pragmatism; prophetic pragmatism and education for creative democracy; and diversity, equality, and creative democracy. Includes a bibliography.

62.    Warner, Linda Sue, and Jimmy Darrell Hastings. "American Indian Education: Culture and Diversity in the 21st Century." Paper presented at the conference on *Culture and Diversity: Teaching, Learning, and the Curriculum for the 21st-century University*, Phoenix, AZ, 7-9 April 1991, ERIC, ED 331664.

Discusses policy trends in American Indian higher education, especially concerning the need to retain Indian value systems and beliefs — as opposed to assimilation into the white culture — and the competition for available funds within the Office of Indian Education Programs. Presents details of the ways by which the diversity and integrity of American Indian education can be enhanced: a larger commitment of federal funds, increased numbers of Indian teachers and administrators, involvement of Indians at all levels of policy development, increasing numbers of students who enter higher education, and a greater utilization of the potential wealth of American Indian nations in land and natural resources. Includes references.

63.    Weiner, Annette B. "Anthropology's Lessons for Cultural Diversity." *The Chronicle of Higher Education* 38 (45) (July 22, 1992): B1-B2.

Gives a brief historical perspective of the growth of anthropology, a discipline generally ignored in the multiculturalism debate but inherently capable of offering much to the discussion. Emphasizes the ways in which anthropology, as a formal area of study, and Franz Boas, its founder, serves to counter at many critical junctures the claims of many who, for example, saw Western civilization as the cultural pinnacle of an upward evolutionary development, impugned the intellectual characteristics and abilities of those less than *100 per cent American,* and ignored the cultural complexity of Native Americans. Argues for more attention to anthropology's understanding of both the need for individuals to maintain multiple cultural identities and the need to utilize a multicultural perspective.

64.    Wiley, Terrence G. "Back From the Past: Prospects and Possibilities for Multicultural Education." *The Journal of General Education* 42 (4) (1993): 280-300.

Addresses several misconceptions and critiques several current models of multicultural education and places this discussion in context of historical perspective. Notes that multiculturalism is not new and is not a single model. Gives examples of early attempts to respond to and control diversity, especially in children's education, language, and immigration. Cites the intercultural education movement of the 1920s and 1930s as anticipatory of some of the stress and conflict today between a common culture and ethnic and cultural diversity. Notes that the social reconstructionist movement of the 1930s that addressed economic inequities and social injustice was attacked similarly for eroding a common ground and creating divisiveness among subgroups. Discusses briefly several contemporary models of multicultural education: (1) teaching the culturally different, (2) the human relations model, (3) the additive approach, (4) single group studies, (5) human diversity models, (6) neosocial reconstructionist approaches, (7) bilingual/bicultural approaches, and (8) ethnonational/ ethnoglobal approaches. Concludes with problems with a *mainstreamcentric* curriculum and the need to become multicultural institutions, not merely institutions that appreciate diversity.

65.    Will, George F. "Multiculturalism Harms Higher Education." In *Education in America: Opposing Viewpoints,* edited by

Charles P. Cozic, 269-275. San Diego: Greenhaven Press, Inc., 1992.

Argues against the encroachment of multiculturalism on traditional-canon territory. Feels that the central danger involved is cultural amnesia rather than cultural hegemony. Disagrees strongly with what he sees as the philosophically primitive and empirically insupportable notion that humanities texts merely reflects social context and, thus, should be read as a political document. Details his argument that not all value judgments are political and that confining categories are condescending and antidemocratic. Defends the need for common ground, for a common thread of national memory, and for the university to serve as transmitters of the cultural legacy that the country needs to define and preserve a sense of national unity regardless of diverse cultural subsets.

66.    Williams, Kenny J. "The Black Studies Syndrome." *Change* 13 (7) (October 1981): 30-37.

Explores the early development of black-studies programs: for example, political aspects, intellectual and academic rigor, selection of professors, and position in the institutional hierarchy. Discusses the early reluctance of many qualified black academicians to become significantly involved because of the possibility of the movement's being only a passing fancy in the sixties and because of a concurrent problem with haphazard curricular scrutiny. Also analyzes the kinds of students involved — or, as the case may be, not involved — during this seminal time. Presents a view of black studies' future and the need for a clear distinction between Afro-American Studies as an academic discipline and as a social answer to current problems.

67.    Wright, Bobby. "American Indian Studies Programs: Surviving the '80s, Thriving in the '90s." *Journal of American Indian Education* 30 (1) (October 1990): 17-24.

Traces the development of American Indian studies programs from the student protests of the late 1960s and early 1970s to the beginning of the 1990s. Looks at academic structure, especially in the context of the expanded, unique roles that these programs often assume: student support services, student recruitment, and affirmative action responsibilities. Analyzes some of the problems faced in both teaching and research in an interdisciplinary field that claims no theory or methodology independent of the established disciplines. Argues, as have proponents of other multicultural studies, for an increased emphasis on a solid intellectual and scholarly base of academic integrity. Offers recommendations for disciplinary growth and enhancement.

68.    Young, Carlene, ed. "An Assessment of Black Studies Programs in American Higher Education." *The Journal of Negro Education* 53 (3) (Summer 1984): 199-378.

Includes articles on imperatives and intellectual questions in Afro-American studies development, global perspectives, black American educational interests in the age of globalism, the unequal status of African studies and Afro-American studies, critical issues in black studies, classification of black studies programs, the legacy of W.E.B. DuBois for contemporary black studies, a plea for greater academic library support, adult education in the black community, the need for black studies scholars to help black students cope with standardized tests, computers and black studies, thematic principles for black studies, and a new role and function of black studies in white and historically black institutions.

# INSTITUTIONAL
# CASE STUDIES

One of the most pragmatically useful elements in the literature on the impact of multiculturalism on higher education is the growing body of information on actual institutional experiences. As an academic exercise alone, case studies give a rich and compelling overview of the birth and growth — sometimes controversial, often sporadic — of curricular and programmatic transformations over the last couple of decades. Beyond general interest and historical understanding, however, these studies can provide both a cautionary tale and a realistic framework to assist others' attempts at similar kinds of institutional change: for example, what to emulate, what to avoid, what kinds of internal institutional reactions to expect, and what guiding philosophies should prove most beneficial.

Even a cursory perusal of the literature highlights the broad range of ways by which higher education has been affected by the components of multiculturalism. Initially striking is the large number of institutions — cutting across typological lines — that have initiated for numerous reasons significant internal changes. Equally striking, however, is the number of larger entities, such as consortiums, philanthropic organizations, and professional associations, that have become active players in the dynamics of multicultural change in the academy. A few examples from the literature can illustrate these points.

Yale University, a private and formerly all-male institution, developed a women's studies program that included new courses and course revisions dedicated to the integration of evolving scholarship into traditional courses. On the other hand, as the first step toward curricular transformation, the University of Southern Maine chose to develop discrete women-focused courses and a separate women's studies curriculum rather than to integrate new scholarship into traditional courses. These two case studies offer an interesting contrast, both in institutional characteristics and in initial responses to a mandate for change.

Two other institutions, one in Virginia and one in Canada, move beyond curricular transformation and illustrate in their respective ways a holistic approach to institutional change. Those in the vanguard for change at Old Dominion University, Norfolk, Virginia, decided that just altering course offerings was not enough. They felt that specific curricular changes must be accompanied by a transformation in educational philosophy, including that which guides the generation of an overall mission statement and the dynamics of strategic planning. The rationale was that effective, successful, long-range transformation could be accomplished only with commitment from those at all levels of responsibility within the university community. Similarly, the University of Lethbridge in Canada decided that along with developing specific courses and a comprehensive Native American studies program, attention must be paid to instituting overall strategies for curricular modification while, at the same time, working diligently to increase the retention of Native American students.

Another comprehensive response is detailed in the case study of the University of Minnesota's "U.S. Cultural Pluralism Requirement." This precedent-setting change goes beyond specialized interdisciplinary ethnic departments and global studies and requires students to complete at least two courses that have a primary focus on African American, Asian American, Native American, and/or Chicano cultures. Other studies look at milestones, such as the tenth-year anniversary of the women's history program at Sarah Lawrence College and the inception of a sweeping preservice and inservice multicultural-education model for both undergraduate and graduate elementary-education teacher preparation at Florida A&M University.

The institutional case-study literature also describes programs that extend beyond regular disciplinary bounds. One such case study describes the mid-1980s success in the growing international-education curriculum components at institutions as diverse as Carleton College, Duke University, Marymount College, Wesleyan University, and Western New England College. Another study describes Mount Holyoke College's Summer Math experience. This six-week residential program for approximately one hundred high school-age women has a social component, as well as the more explicit orientation toward mathematics fundamentals, computer programming, and applications functions. One final example of multiculturalism extending beyond the curriculum is found at the University of Wisconsin-Madison's library, which has been building a women's studies reading area. This case study describes the budget and personnel involved, the librarian's role, and the composition of the collection.

Another aspect of change is detailed in studies that present the results of projects on a scope beyond that of single institutions. One such case study describes the creation and progress of the Western States Project on Women in the Curriculum, one of the first large-scale networks to provide seed money, resources, training, and technical assistance to a number of campuses. Another study examines the impact of the Southwest Institute for Research on Women at the University of Arizona. This three-year project promoted a dialogue between leaders in women's studies and those in international studies. The case study itself describes the resultant impact of the overall experience on faculty at institutions in Arizona, Colorado, New Mexico, and Utah.

Two other studies illustrate the range and significance of large-scale projects. The first reviews specific classroom and course changes resulting from integration work generated from participation in the New Jersey Project on Gender Integration. Among other goals, this statewide initiative addressed the practical task of altering research methods courses to integrate gender and race into the curriculum. The study focuses on one institution, Ramapo College, where there was a forceful emphasis on striving toward both intellectual validity in all new courses and integration across the widest possible curricular spectrum. The second study describes institutional projects that share the primary goal of integrating knowledge about white women and women and men of color into the curriculum by developing new courses or revising traditional ones.

Beyond the front lines of academe itself, both philanthropic and professional organizations have become involved in the changes engendered by the multicultural movement. The Ford Foundation, for instance, implemented a multiyear program to aid in developing and institutionalizing women's studies by attempting to change the formal postsecondary undergraduate core curricula. This case study examines ·the issues, challenges, and strategies involved in this large program, focusing briefly on specific projects at eleven institutions, including the University of California at Los Angeles, Duke University, the University of Arizona, Columbia University, and the University of Oregon. Similarly, the Association of American Colleges initiated a project to coordinate a network of colleges and universities that would design programs of common study introducing students to multiple cultures. A major goal of this alliance was to produce a curriculum that would win widespread support from faculty across disciplinary lines, from departmental levels, and from students.

The examples above are only a small cross section of the rich literature available on case studies. Taken both individually and collectively, these studies provide a fascinating view of the continuum of change in higher education in the last third of the twentieth century. They also, of course, can provide valuable practical information for those interested in initiating similar new programs or expanding, revising, or refining existing curricular components.

## Institutional Case Studies

69.    Bazin, Nancy Topping. "Transforming the Curriculum, The Mission Statement, The Strategic Goals: A Success Story." *Initiatives* 54 (1) (Spring 1991): 39-46.

Details the extensive curricular changes undergone at Old Dominion University (public, enrolling approximately 16,000), where since 1986 general education requirements have included the perspectives, contributions, and concerns of women, minorities, and/or non-Western cultures. In a larger sense, discusses the school's impressive transformation in educational philosophy, including a revision in both the mission statement and the dynamics of strategic planning. Explains the development of a comprehensive, broad base of acceptance by those who must initiate, defend, and implement such fundamental changes: from the State Council of Higher Education to the faculty. Presents some of the specific changes that have occurred and some of the problems that still must be confronted. Defends the notion that such progress in implementing the goal of diversity in what is taught, who does the teaching, and who is being taught requires not only changes in curricula, but also changes in an institution's overall commitment to multiculturalism at all levels of responsibility.

70. Beaty, Jeanna, and Katherine Beaty Chiste. "University Preparation for Native American Students: Theory and Application." *Journal of American Indian Education* 26 (1) (October 1986): 6-13.

Discusses the approach of a Canadian institution, the University of Lethbridge, to the increasing demands of both a growing Native American student population and a desire to develop more fully a Native American studies program. Describes the institution's University Preparation Program to improve retention and graduation rates and the attempts to fashion a curriculum based on a holistic model that balances the cognitive, affective, and psychomotoric aspects of knowledge acquisition. Explains some of the unique components of "Indianness" and applies this knowledge to strategies for developing or modifying curricular and teaching methodologies. Examines the institution's evaluation of the program's aims and some of the attendant problems and overall implications.

71. Betteridge, Anne, and Janice Monk. "Teaching Women's Studies from an International Perspective." *Women's Studies Quarterly* 18 (1 & 2) (Spring/Summer 1990): 78-85.

Examines the results of a three-year (1987-90) project initiated by the Southwest Institute for Research on Women at the University of Arizona and dedicated to promoting a dialogue between leaders in women's studies and those in international studies. Focuses on the five major elements of the project: (1) intensive summer institutes to provide resources, (2) a subsequent period of independent work to build bibliographies, (3) regional work-in-progress meetings, (4) new course design and implementation, and (5) dissemination of project materials. Looks at the project's success in assisting women's studies faculty in Arizona, Colorado, New Mexico, and Utah to develop international perspectives in pedagogy. Also examines some of the continuing challenges and presents a selected bibliography.

72.    Bolsterli, Margaret Jones. "Teaching Women's Studies at the University of Arkansas." In *Stepping off the Pedestal: Academic Women in the South*, edited by Patricia A. Stringer and Irene Thompson, 71-75. New York: The Modern Language Association of America, 1982.

Relates the extremely slow and grudging acceptance in the late 1970s and early 1980s at the University of Arkansas, Fayetteville, of specific courses related to women (*Women and Modern Literature* and *The Female in Contemporary America*) and the generally apathetic campus attitude, even of female students, concerning women's issues. Describes attempts to engage faculty, department, and student interest in an atmosphere where feminism is disparaged and where Scarlett O'Hara was frequently listed by women students as the only fictional character they have ever come across that they would like to emulate. Discusses also, however, the extremely small, but slowly growing, cadre of students deeply interested in exploring and understanding women's perspectives. Gives examples of both disheartening failures and relatively minor, but deeply encouraging, successes.

73.    Buford, Carmen. "Multicultural Programming in a University Women's Center." *Initiatives* 51 (2 & 3) (Summer 1988): 31-35.

Presents a rationale for the existence of a campus women's center, especially given the increasingly pluralistic nature of higher education and the growing emphasis on multiculturalism in the curriculum. Uses the center at California State University, Dominguez Hills, as a specific example. Discusses the five stages that people other than Anglo must go through to come to terms with what is perceived as a racist and Eurocentric society in the United States. Also details the ways in which this center holistically tries to aid this development. Includes descriptions of various programs, many not normally provided elsewhere on campus; of the multicultural nature of the syllabus for a formal course offering; of the help provided for older women students; and of the role that the larger institution must play in assisting the birth and growth of such programs.

74.  Butler, Johnnella E. "Complicating the Question: Black Studies and Women's Studies." In *Women's Place in the Academy: Transforming the Liberal Arts Curriculum*, edited by Marilyn R. Schuster and Susan R. Van Dyne, 73-86. Totowa, NJ: Rowman and Allanheld, 1985.

Describes an early 1980s faculty-development project funded by the Fund for the Improvement of Postsecondary Education that brought together 20 faculty members from 5 colleges — University of Massachussetts- Amherst, Amherst, Hampshire, Mount Holyoke, and Smith — to examine the intersections of black studies and women's studies. Cites issues and perspectives the two held in common while acknowledging the biases and blind spots of each field. Gives an overview of the goals and products of the workshop and shares examples of faculty conflict during the workshop, emanating from cultural differences in communication and interaction. Concludes with a brief description of a course, *Teaching Women and Philosophy*, that the author developed with a colleague as part of the two-year project.

75.  Clarey, Joanne H. "Integrating Integration Methods with Women's Studies: The University of Southern Maine's Experience." In *Toward Excellence and Equity: The Scholarship on Women as a Catalyst for Change in the University*, edited by JoAnn M. Fritsche, 209-213. Orono, ME: University of Maine at Orono, 1985.

Explains the University of Southern Maine's decision to begin curricular reform by developing discrete women-focused courses and a women's studies curriculum as the first stage to transformation, rather than beginning by integrating into the existing curriculum. Discusses the rationale of needing an educational process and opportunity that can help develop equal strengths, of providing specific cross-cultural and historical perspectives, and of helping women to reconstruct and restore the past. Examines the departmental-team approach adopted for implementation and the methods of general course revision. Reports on evaluative results, mostly positive. Looks, also, at some problems and some thoughts about the future, concerning both the existing women's studies methods of transformation and the integrative methods that should follow.

76.    Cott, Nancy F. "The Women's Studies Program: Yale University." In *Toward A Balanced Curriculum: A Sourcebook for Initiating Gender Integration Projects*, edited by Bonnie B. Spanier, Alexander Bloom, and Darlene Boroviak, 91-97. Cambridge, MA: Schenkman Publishing Company, Inc., 1984.

Describes the 1981 development of a major in women's studies at Yale University by the women's studies program. Includes information on a faculty development seminar that extended over two years and was key to the development of new courses and course revisions. Explains the double strategy of new courses with a specific focus on women and the integration of new scholarship and perspectives into traditional courses. Briefly reviews seven standard lecture courses and gives examples of changes in content, organization, and titles. Shows how involvement may extend beyond the customary women's studies faculty, who most often were female and untenured, and how wider involvement brings greater prestige to women's studies and acceptance of change.

77.    Crawley, Donna, and Martha Ecker. "Integrating Issues of Gender, Race, and Ethnicity into Experimental Psychology and Other Social-Science Methodology Courses." *Women's Studies Quarterly* 18 (1 & 2) (Spring/Summer 1990): 105-116.

Addresses the practical task of altering research-methods courses to integrate gender and race into the curriculum and examines the concomitant difficulties attending such an endeavor. Reviews specific classroom and course settings that resulted from integration work generated from

participation in the New Jersey Project on Gender
Integration. Presents theoretical (e.g., the nature of
knowledge) and practical considerations that shaped the
project's translation into reality at Ramapo College. Discusses
the need to emphasize strongly both the intellectual validity
of these courses and the need for integrating the women's
perspective across the widest possible curricular spectrum.

78.    Dinnerstein, Myra, and others. "Reports on Curriculum
       Integration Projects." *Women's Studies Quarterly* 13 (2)
       (Summer 1985): 17-22.

       Details the dynamics of a number of specific programs
at either the institutional or group level. Includes such
specifics as inception, relative level of growth and impact,
curricular description, extracurricular offerings, faculty
response to changes, funding, and successes and
disappointments. Shows the positive influence of large
external entities (e.g., the National Endowment for the
Humanities and the Ford Foundation) on the birth and
development of curriculum-integration projects. Includes the
following colleges, universities, and groups: Arizona,
Carleton, Colgate, Great Lakes Colleges Association,
University of Illinois at Chicago, Lewis & Clark, New
Mexico, Organization of American Historians, Spelman,
Towson State, and University of Texas at El Paso.

79.    Edwards, Jane. "Rhetoric and Pragmatism in International
       Education." *Liberal Education* 73 (4) (September/October
       1987): 22-33.

       Discusses the discernible, but slow, growth of
international education curricular components. Analyzes
some of the most significant problems that accompany an
academic area that is frequently affected by prevailing
political fashions that often are characterized by the failure
even to reach a consensus on the meaning of such
fundamental terms as cross-cultural, multicultural,
intercultural, and global. Includes a look at some of the most
current notions about international education and then

attempts to define a pragmatic agenda for curricular implementation of what often are extraordinarily fragmented courses, disciplines, and programs. Presents case studies of curricular integration at five institutions (Carleton College, Duke University, Marymount College, Wesleyan University, and Western New England College) and within one consortium (Southwest Institute for Research on Women), all having relative success on a number of levels.

80.    Foss, Karen A. "Cultivating the Cracks: Using Existing Structures to Implement a Feminist Agenda." *CUPA Journal* (Summer 1993): 61-63.

Cites two fundamental ways that feminists may bring about change: working to change actual structures and working within the existing institutional structures. Notes the importance of full-professor status to give legitimacy to women's issues and ideas. Based on 16 years of experience at Humboldt State University, gives four examples of advancing feminist issues and thought by working within traditional structures: (1) institutionalizing courses with a feminist perspective (e.g., a course on gender and communication), (2) serving on university personnel committees (e.g., promotion and tenure), (3) developing leadership in a women's studies program, and (4) addressing feminist concerns in public address.

81.    Frank, Shirley, ed. "Transforming the Traditional Curriculum: A Special Feature." *Women's Studies Quarterly* 10 (1) (Spring 1982): 19-48.

Includes articles on the integration of women's studies into the larger curriculum, curriculum integration at the University of Arizona, the integration of the study of women into the liberal arts at Wheaton College, curriculum revision and women's equity at Montana State University, the extent of the new scholarship on women, and a *WARNING: The New Scholarship on Women May Be Hazardous to Your Ego.*

82. Gussman, Deborah, and Wendy Hesford. "A Dialogical Approach to Teaching Introductory Women's Studies." *Feminist Teacher* 6 (3) (Spring 1992): 32-39.

Describes an interdisciplinary development of a revised women's studies introductory course at Rutgers University. Presents the underlying assumption that to understand feminist inquiry, the process of learning must be fundamentally revised and seen more as autobiographic, revisionist, and dialogic. Defines these terms as they relate to the course and describes in detail the ways by which students conducted dialogues with texts, with other students in a collaborative process, and with teachers. Includes an extensive reference list.

83. Hedges, Elaine, and others. "Towson State University Community College Curriculum Transformation Project." *Women's Studies Quarterly* 18 (1 & 2) (Spring/Summer 1990): 122-125.

Examines an ongoing project involving five community colleges in Maryland (completed in the spring of 1990). Was one of the few at that time attempting to address the needs of community colleges, which routinely enroll over one-third of all students in higher education. Involved forty-five faculty members meeting in workshops to study the new scholarship on women, modify existing courses and standard pedagogy, and test these changes in actual classrooms. Organized participating faculty by campus and by discipline or subject area before their participation in one of five workshops that formed the heart of the project: (1) biology/ allied health, (2) fine arts, (3) history/philosophy, (4) literature/composition, and (5) social sciences (psychology, sociology, and business). Emphasized both intracampus and intercampus collegiality and cooperation for maximum effectiveness. Details specific changes that were generated as a result of the project, plus an analysis of overall student demographics. Explains the long-term goals of both establishing a statewide network through which curriculum transformation could be more fully institutionalized and addressing the technical/career curriculum that the original project only partially addressed.

84.    Hill, Leslie I. "The Ford Foundation Program on Mainstreaming Minority Women's Studies." *Women's Studies Quarterly* 18 (1 & 2) (Spring/Summer 1990): 24-38.

Describes the Ford Foundation's still-evolving program to aid in developing and institutionalizing women's studies by attempting to change the formal postsecondary undergraduate core curricula. Assesses the issues and challenges faced and the strategies devised to deal with them. Presents the salient points of a June 1989 National Council for Research on Women meeting of project directors. Offers abstracts of projects at eleven institutions and includes contact names and addresses for each: Barnard College; University of California, Los Angeles; Duke University; University of Arizona; Memphis State University; George Washington University; City University of New York Graduate School and University Center; Columbia University; Metropolitan State University; University of Oregon; University of Wisconsin-Madison.

85.    Hoffman, Nancy. "Black Studies, Ethnic Studies and Women's Studies: Some Reflections on Collaborative Projects." *Women's Studies Quarterly* 14 (1 & 2) (Spring/Summer 1986): 49-57.

Describes institutional projects that share the primary and public goal of integrating knowledge about white women and women and men of color into the curriculum by developing new courses or revising traditional ones. Reflects on ultimate results and then analyzes the circumstances that precipitated the inception of these projects and the attendant problems. Extrapolates from individual and collective experiences to some general principles. Gives an overview, plus an analysis of other appropriate key elements (e.g., history, philosophy, impact, and approach), for each of the projects. Includes names and addresses for contacts at California State Polytechnic University, Smith College,

University of Massachusetts, William Paterson College, Memphis State University, University of Illinois at Chicago, San Francisco State University, and Spelman College.

86.  Jesudason, Melba. "Building a Women's Studies Reading Area Collection: University of Wisconsin-Madison, College Library Experience." *Reference Services Review* 20 (1) (Spring 1992): 81-93.

Presents the background, and a brief history, of the women's studies reading area collection at the University of Wisconsin-Madison (UWM). Reviews the literature on the disciplinary nature of women's studies and on a women's studies library collection as part of the collection development in academic libraries, specifically as a category of special collection. Describes a conceptual model for a women's studies collection based on a curricular integration project; uses the Women's Studies Reading Area Collection at UWM as an example. Analyzes budget, personnel, librarian's role, and collection composition. Also presents an alphabetical listing of "Women's File Subject Heading" and a list and discussion of tools that can assist in the maintenance of such a special collection.

87.  Langland, Elizabeth. "Women's Studies at Vanderbilt: Toward a Strategy for the Eighties." In *Stepping off the Pedestal: Academic Women in the South,* edited by Patricia A. Stringer and Irene Thompson, 41-47. New York: The Modern Language Association of America, 1982.

Looks at the birth and development of the women's studies program at Vanderbilt, a highly respected private university that did not have a tradition of high female enrollments in its College of Arts and Science until the early 1980s. Details some of the initial — and some continuing — problems that were confronted and explores the profound impact of a late-1970s symposium that brought to the campus major figures in women's studies. Assesses the evolution of strategies that were developed to overcome problems and deal with basic issues. Presents four components of a plan to ensure the growing success of the program.

88.     McIntosh, Peggy, Katherine Stanis, and Barbara Kneubuh, comps. "Transforming the Liberal Arts Curriculum through Incorporation of the New Scholarship on Women." *Women's Studies Quarterly* 11 (2) (Summer 1983): 4-36.

Along with articles on terminology and a working definition of a balanced course, includes articles on a Skidmore College conference (Toward a Nonsexist Education), women's studies as a catalyst for change at the College of New Rochelle women's college, the ten-year anniversary of the women's history program at Sarah Lawrence college, the formation of new connections at the University of New Hampshire, and the first women's studies course at Georgia Southern College (now Georgia Southern University).

89.     Meacham, John A. "Guiding Principles for Development and Implementation of Multicultural Courses." *The Journal of General Education* 42 (4) (1993): 301-315.

Discusses the revised undergraduate curriculum at the State University of New York-Buffalo and describes two courses that address diversity: *World Civilization* and *American Pluralism*. Gives a brief description of each course and then provides 10 principles for the design and implementation of multicultural core courses: (1) use a broad range of content and issues to address diversity, (2) use faculty expertise in course design, (3) consider teaching styles and the interaction between course content and student expectation, (4) offer faculty development programs, (5) establish moderate goals for student learning, (6) listen to concerns, (7) pilot and evaluate multicultural courses, (8) keep faculty expectations modest, (9) keep the process of course design open, and (10) publicize new courses. Notes that the demographic argument of change was the most effective in building support for the courses.

90.    Mercer, Walter A. "The Florida A&M University Preservice and Inservice Multicultural Education Model." *The Negro Educational Review* 34 (1) (January 1983): 37-44.

Defends the need for a much larger, sharper focus on multicultural education at all levels. Describes the efforts of the National Coalition for Cultural Pluralism to define some specific goals that can aid in achieving an educational atmosphere conducive to multiculturalism. Shows how a conference entitled, *The Future of Multicultural Instructional Materials*, sponsored by the National Education Association and the Council on Interracial Books for Children, further defined both the need for and the goals of pluralism through education. Presents the multicultural-education model for Florida A&M University's preservice and in-service programs in undergraduate and graduate elementary-education teacher training. Includes, for example, objectives; selection and organization principles; instructional materials; description of the in-service seminar; and planning, implementation, and evaluative timelines.

91.    Mooney, Carolyn J. "Amid the Continuing Debate over 'Political Correctness,' University of Arizona Courses Seek to Explore the Middle Ground." *The Chronicle of Higher Education* 37 (37) (May 29, 1991): A9-A10.

Describes *Critical Concepts in Western Culture*, a new series of humanities courses at the University of Arizona, that attempts to strike a reasonable balance between the polarizing elements in the political-correctness debate. Discusses the apparent success of this approach that still examines ideas associated with Western civilization but does so from numerous other cultural perspectives. Notes that the objective has switched from mere understanding to understanding coupled with comparative critiques. Describes attempts by some faculty to establish a department of cultural studies and explains the current charges that have transpired in traditional requirements, overall perspective, and pedagogy. Includes a brief examination of course format and requirements and grading, plus a selection of suggested readings.

92.     Morris, Paula. "Increasing Awareness: A Multifaceted Approach." In *Toward Excellence and Equity: The Scholarship on Women as a Catalyst for Change in the University*, edited by JoAnn M. Fritsche, 214-218. Orono, ME: University of Maine at Orono, 1985.

Discusses the pilot project and follow-up results of a curriculum-integration project, both efforts predicated on an awareness of the need for a multifaceted and incremental approach to change. Presents a year-by-year analysis of the variety of people and methods utilized for curricular change and at the ways in which one change could logically lead to another. Assesses the value and impact of the project's three major components — a study group, guest-speaker and consultant presentations, and faculty research projects — and details some of the resultant specific course revisions.

93.     Morros, Lucy. "Moving Toward a Balanced Curriculum at a Small Independent College," In *Toward Excellence and Equity: The Scholarship on Women as a Catalyst for Change in the University*, edited by JoAnn M. Fritsche, 188-192. Orono, ME: University of Maine at Orono, 1985.

Details the growth at Westbrook College of a 1982 initiative to revise courses so that they would focus on the contributions, values, and perspectives of both men and women. Provides an intellectual and historical justification for a greater inclusion of women's perspectives in a higher-education curriculum. Examines faculty development efforts and the impact of revision on nursing, a specific degree program that is generally considered outside the core areas of women's studies (e.g., literature, history, art, and the social sciences). Summarizes the college's continued move toward a balanced curriculum, including some of the hurdles still remaining.

94. Morrow, Charlene, and James Morrow. "Whose Math is it Anyway? Giving Girls a Chance to Take Charge of Their Math Learning." *Initiatives* 55 (3) (1993): 49-59.

> Describes the structure and success over the past 10 years of Mount Holyoke College's Summer Math, a 6-week program for approximately 100 high school-age women. Briefly summarizes the current state of mathematics education for women and presents some of the program's guiding principles, based largely on consistent findings from the research literature about how women can be successful in mathematics classrooms. Describes the three major academic components — fundamental mathematical concepts, computer programming, and mathematical applications — and the value of the residential social component. Presents the goals and results of the program and offers both suggestions for reform and strategies that have proven beneficial over the program's history.

95. National Council for Research on Women. *Mainstreaming Minority Women's Studies.* New York: National Council for Research on Women, 1991. 32 pp.

> Begun in 1989, this Ford Foundation project enabled 13 women's research centers to collaborate with ethnic studies programs and with minority scholars to develop curriculum integration models. At the center was the goal to advance research and teaching about women of color and to integrate this scholarship into the undergraduate curricula. Participants included Arizona, Barnard College, University of California-Los Angeles, Wisconsin-Madison, George Washington, Columbia, Duke/North Carolina-Chapel Hill, Memphis State, Metropolitan State, City University of New York, University at Albany-SUNY, and Oregon.

96. O'Barr, Jean F. *Feminism in Action: Building Institutions and Community through Women's Studies.* Chapel Hill, NC: The University of North Carolina Press, 1994. 301 pp.

Explores a dynamic process of feminist institution building — psychological, physical, and intellectual — based on over 20 years of the author's experience in listening, explaining, teaching, and organizing at Duke University. Using many examples throughout, focuses on the need for women's studies, the origins of women's studies, and understanding women's diversities and commonalities. Gives specific examples of curriculum transformation, student learning, feminist thought, and the transformation of knowledge. Concludes with chapters on fundraising, journal publication, and women's studies as a discipline. Believes that women's studies should continue both as a discipline and an interdisciplinary field.

97.     Ognibene, Elaine R. "Integrating the Curriculum: From Impossible to Possible." *College Teaching* 37 (3) (Summer 1989): 105-110.

Presents a synopsis of a special 1988 program sponsored by the Faculty Committee on College Teaching at Siena College, New York, and stimulated by the continuing work to establish an interdisciplinary approach to curriculum integration. Focuses on (1) explaining the fundamental theory behind integration as opposed to the commonly held belief that integration involves simply adding readings and (2) showing what faculty were actually doing in their classes, hoping to offer prescriptive, corrective models. Calls for radical, rather than token or cosmetic, changes and presents discussions of four specific areas — political science, religious studies, English, and perspectives on *Women and Minorities* — that can serve as models. Discusses the evolutionary nature of Siena's evaluative procedures.

98.     Paige-Pointer, Barbara, and Gale Schroeder Auletta. "Restructuring the Curriculum: Barriers and Bridges." *Women's Studies Quarterly* 18 (1 & 2) (Spring/Summer 1990): 86-94.

Assesses a 1984 chancellor's grant, *Mainstreaming Cross-Cultural Perspectives into the Curriculum*, to California State

University, Hayward, to restructure the curriculum and increase faculty awareness of the increasing need for change because of shifting student demographics. Discusses the project's structure and design, predicated on the need to (1) encourage voluntary faculty participation, (2) take advantage of existing multicultural resources on campus, (3) address areas of resistance and apathy, and (4) develop tangible resources and a support network. Includes a discussion of the use of departmental coordinators, who played a critical role in countering resistance or apathy. Also includes a list of materials generated as a direct result of the project. Comments both on the realistic modesty of the initial successes and, at the same time, the program's positive future.

99. Rothenberg, Paula. "The New Jersey Project Enters Its Second Phase." *Women's Studies Quarterly* 18 (1 & 2) (Spring/Summer 1990): 119-122.

Traces the development since its inception in 1986 of the New Jersey Project, the first statewide, multiyear curriculum transformation project in the nation. Looks at some of the accomplishments of the three-year period initially funded by the state's Department of Higher Education and then presents some of the desired goals that may be reached because of an additional three years of funding. Includes a discussion of such project components as continuing support and resources for faculty who are currently involved in curricular transformation; encouragement of greater faculty participation; collaboration with a newly funded multiyear, statewide *Multicultural Studies Project*; regional network meetings; statewide workshops; a new student-achievement award for excellence in feminist scholarship; encouragement of greater curricular integration in mathematics, science, and technology; and development of academic alliances between higher education and secondary schools. Provides contact names and numbers and a look at one particular example of project implementation: the *Towson State University Community College Curriculum Transformation Project*.

100.    Schmitz, Betty. "Project on Women in the Curriculum:
        Montana State University." In *Toward A Balanced Curriculum:
        A Sourcebook for Initiating Gender Integration Projects*, edited by
        Bonnie B. Spanier, Alexander Bloom, and Darlene Boroviak,
        80-90. Cambridge, MA: Schenkman Publishing Company,
        Inc., 1984.

        Describes the Montana State University Project, funded
        by the Women's Educational Equity Act, aimed at curricular
        reform. Describes how participants were selected and how a
        previous interest in sex bias influenced involvement. Also
        points to the importance of a stipend for participation. Gives
        an overview of the activities during the two-year project
        period. Describes the three types of curricular reform: new
        courses or course revisions, textbook assessment and the
        development of guidelines for the inclusion of women, and
        research on nontraditional students. Shows also that the
        project had the intended effect of broadening the
        participants' attitudes toward women's rights and roles.
        Summarizes key findings from the ten projects involved in
        the Northern Rockies Program on Women in the Curriculum.

101.    Schmitz, Betty, Myra Dinnerstein, and Nancy Mairs.
        "Initiating a Curriculum Integration Project: Lessons from the
        Campus and the Region." In *Women's Place in the Academy:
        Transforming the Liberal Arts Curriculum*, edited by Marilyn R.
        Schuster and Susan R. Van Dyne, 116-129. Totowa, NJ:
        Rowman and Allanheld, 1985.

        Compares the initiation and development of curricular-
        change projects at Montana State University and the
        University of Arizona, two of the first institutions to expose
        non-women's studies faculty to feminist scholarship.
        Examines the effective, but different, methods by which the
        two project leaders chose participants and the effective, and
        similar, results that were apparent after outcomes were
        measured. Assesses the various levels of resistance to
        feminist scholarship among faculty and the ways by which
        project participants deflected criticism or intellectual
        antagonism. Also describes the later development of the

Northern Rockies Program on Women in the Curriculum, one of the first holistic networks to provide seed money, resources, training, and technical assistance to, in this case, ten campuses in Idaho, Montana, Utah, and Wyoming. Looks, too, at the Western States Project on Women in the Curriculum, another collective extension of the Montana State and Arizona projects. Presents a model for designing a successful program.

102. Schneider, Carol G. "Exploring the Complexities of Culture." *Liberal Education* 77 (3) (May/June 1991): 40-60.

Presents some of the most important results of the first two years of an Association of American Colleges project to coordinate a network of colleges and universities designing programs of common study to introduce students to the study of multiple cultures. Emphasizes that the challenges of the project — called *Engaging Cultural Legacies: Shaping Core Curriculum in the Humanities* — are to shape a curriculum that can win widespread support from faculty members, departments, and students and to encourage colleges and universities that accept this challenge to confront the intellectual and institutional task of determining what such a commitment means in the evolution of American, Western, and world history. Looks at the way in which many institutions are combining concepts from both the humanities and the social sciences. Describes salient strategies used by clusters of specific programs throughout the nation (includes contact names and addresses and sample syllabi). Also includes a complete list of institutions (with contact persons) participating in the project: Fairleigh Dickinson, Trenton State College, University of Wyoming, SUNY-Buffalo, Fisk University, Mount Holyoke College, CUNY-Queens College, Tufts University, University of Oklahoma, University of Denver, Queens College, Mount Saint Mary's College; CUNY-Brooklyn College, Columbia, Earlham, University of North Carolina-Asheville.

103.    Spanier, Bonnie B. "Toward A Balanced Curriculum: The
        Study of Women at Wheaton College." *Change* 14 (3) (April
        1982): 31-34.

        Explores the dynamics and the impact of a federally
        funded program begun in 1980 to integrate women's
        experiences into the curricular mainstream and to bring a
        gender-balanced perspective to the traditional liberal arts at
        Wheaton, a small, liberal arts women's college. Discusses the
        need for a balance between the new and the older, traditional
        scholarship about women. Describes the positive impact of
        an initial faculty retreat that was held to, for example,
        pinpoint major issues, assess the role of ideology in the
        curriculum, and formulate appropriate strategies. Notes
        some of the changes that have occurred, using the
        psychology department as a specific example. Looks, also, at
        student response and lists some essential ingredients that
        Wheaton's experience imply are necessary for a successful
        transformation.

104.    Spanier, Bonnie B. "Toward A Balanced Curriculum:
        Wheaton College." In *Toward A Balanced Curriculum: A
        Sourcebook for Initiating Gender Integration Projects*, edited by
        Bonnie B. Spanier, Alexander Bloom, and Darlene Boroviak,
        73-79. Cambridge, MA: Schenkman Publishing Company,
        Inc., 1984.

        Analyzes some of the specific curricular changes at
        Wheaton College four years after the initiation of a project to
        integrate women's perspectives into its liberal arts
        curriculum. Portrays the project model as both top-down
        because of the administrative initiative involved and bottom-
        up because conditions were created to stimulate faculty
        interest in, and knowledge about, the new scholarship about
        women. Presents and explains the three key elements in
        Wheaton's approach and analyzes the impact of the
        integration on the curriculum. Comments, also, on the
        significance of the outside funding that was the formal
        impetus for the resultant integration effort. Offers
        suggestions for others, even those who may not be suitable

candidates for such a comprehensive approach as Wheaton took.

105.     Stringer, Patricia A., and Irene Thompson, eds. *Stepping Off the Pedestal: Academic Women in the South.* New York: The Modern Language Association of America, 1982. 181 pp.

Divides the essays into three sections: (1) the mythology of where we've been, (2) examining the myth (women's studies in the South — Vanderbilt, Old Dominion, Arkansas, and Mississippi), and (3) confronting the myth and where we're going (case studies from Harvard and the University of Florida, as well as the myths of the *doubly burdened* and the *doubly blessed* status of the black female academic. Includes four other essays and a bibliographical essay on the historical perspective.

106.     Swedberg, Gertrude L. "Gender Balancing the Curriculum with Faculty/Student Teamwork: A Case Study." Paper presented at the Annual Meeting of the National Women's Studies Association, Minneapolis, 22 June 1988. ERIC, ED 303392.

Discusses the results of a five-year pilot project initiated at Eastern Washington University in 1983 to integrate women's scholarship into traditional disciplines. Gives details about involved personnel (faculty, the curriculum committee, resource persons, and library personnel), methods of coordination, and results (assessments of traditional scholarship, generation of new materials, and classroom interaction). Presents specific curricular changes, as well as a brief discussion of the development of (1) a brochure describing the project, (2) project materials that were placed in binders for university departments, and (3) initiation of a feminist-theory research program series.

107.     Update: Association News and Developments in Higher Education. "Amid Controversy, Texas Postpones Multicultural Syllabus." *Academe* 76 (6) (November/ December 1990): 5-6.

Gives some background on the controversial multiculturally based composition syllabus at the University of Texas. Discusses the expressed aims of the original revision's call for a unified syllabus: examining the differences between opinion and argument and integrating multicultural education into the undergraduate curriculum. Examines some of the criticism that led to the postponement and the debate's burgeoning attention in national, as well as local, media. Looks, also, at some of the continuing support for the change and some of the organizational responses to the controversy.

108.   Zita, Jacquelyn. "From Orthodoxy to Pluralism: A Postsecondary Curricular Reform." *Journal of Education* 170 (2) (1988): 58-76.

Describes the University of Minnesota's precedent-setting *U.S. Cultural Pluralism Requirement*, which goes beyond specialized interdisciplinary ethnic departments and global studies and requires all undergraduates to complete at least two courses that have a primary focus on Afro-American, Asian-American, American Indian, and/or Chicano cultures. Examines the basics of the reform, including a continual assessment of the criteria, terminology problems, and the development of a compelling rationale for making these courses required. Groups into five categories the recurrent themes of the arguments and debates that surrounded the requirement's passage and implementation and offers an analysis and refutation of each. Looks, finally, at the overall positive effects and advantages of the adoption of such a requirement.

# TRADITIONAL DISCIPLINES
# AND INTERDISCIPLINARY FIELDS

This chapter focuses on curricular changes across higher education in traditional disciplines and in interdisciplinary fields. Because the overall emphasis of this research is on women's studies, African-American studies, ethnic studies, and international education, works descriptive of changes in these fields are documented throughout this publication; therefore, the annotations for these fields in this section are primarily limited to books that review the emerging fields from a holistic perspective.

## Black Studies

The status of black studies in the academy and issues central to this field of inquiry are the focus of several books. *Introduction to Afro-American Studies: A Peoples College Primer* started as a course syllabus-study guide in 1973 at Fisk University. Published in 1986, this text begins with an overview of the who, what, why, and for whom of Afro-American studies and goes on to describe historical events and current issues central to the black experience in America. Emphasis is given, for example, to the black middle class, black culture, religion and black churches, education and the school in the black community, civil rights and the struggle for democracy, and present and future roles for blacks.

*Black Studies: Theory, Method and Cultural Perspectives*, issued in 1990 and edited by Talmadge Anderson, includes an interdisciplinary collection of essays focusing on an emerging paradigm in black studies and appropriate research frameworks (an issue also important in women's studies), along with sections on African-American history, sociological perspectives, blacks and politics, psychology and the Afrocentric ethos, and black economic perspectives. In 1993, Talmadge authored *Introduction to African American Studies: Cultural Concepts and Theory*, a concise and informative volume covering the foundation, philosophy, and issues of African-American studies. In a short volume, *Black Studies,*

*Rap and the Academy*, Baker (1993) presents a brief history of black studies, its vitality and health, and prospects for the discipline in the late 1990s.

In combination, these books provide a comprehensive overview of black studies: historical context, current content and issues, methodologies, and future needs. The resonant chord is the broad perspective of the field and the many fronts that need sustained scholarly attention. Certainly, small programs with limited numbers of scholars are challenged by the vast array of content to study and research, the responsibility for teaching black studies to students both within and outside of the field, and the "required" involvement with a growing number of political issues (e.g., affirmative action and speech codes) on campus and beyond. Alan Colon in an article in the *Journal of Negro Education* notes that further development of black studies to cover the many areas of need will require a multifaceted approach, including historically white institutions, historically black institutions, and, importantly, community-based alternative institutions, each performing in its uniquely effective way. This conclusion seems most appropriate.

## International Education

International or global education has many dimensions and is practiced through a wide variety of programs and activities on college campuses. A 1991 study by the Association of American Colleges found that area studies and issues courses are two important dimensions of international education. Courses on Eastern and Western Europe, Anglo-America, and Latin America predominated in area studies while diplomacy and environment led in global-issues courses. Other broad issue categories include food, international trade and finance, intelligence and communications, medical studies, peace studies, population, and natural resources. The diversity in these issues suggests that courses with an international focus may be found in any discipline, and some disciplines have formed these studies into degree-granting programs, for example, international business, international or comparative education, and international agriculture.

Two valuable books, however, address the need for integration of international perspectives across all disciplines.

*Group Portrait: Internationalizing the Disciplines*, edited by Sven Groennings and David Wiley, reviews seven disciplines (geography, history, political science, sociology, psychology, journalism and mass communication, and philosophy) and calls for university and college curricula to be aware of the growing significance of intercultural contexts. In the edited volume *International Master Modules for Internationalizing the Curriculum: A General Catalogue*, short summaries of more than 175 International Master Modules, encompassing over 60 disciplines and subject areas, are provided. Plus, a rationale for developing classes in international studies and introducing international components into existing classes is reviewed. These two books are useful resources for curricular integration projects aimed at incorporating international dimensions into traditional courses of study.

International study is also achieved through study abroad, foreign language studies and instruction, and faculty development efforts. International education has in common with African-American studies and women's studies the planning and implementation of many activities that go beyond traditional courses and programs to achieve educational and institutional objectives.

Academicians generally acknowledge the emerging world economy, the global environment, and, consequently, at least in supposition, the need for increased attention to international education. Questions of race and gender, and their place in academe, that are raised by women's studies and African-American studies receive less support and often are under attack.

## Women's Studies

Johnnella Butler, a leading scholar in the field of women's studies and ethnic studies, along with John C. Walter, provides an incisive view of issues that surround the intersections of gender, race, and culture in the academy in the edited volume *Transforming the Curriculum: Ethnic Studies and Women's Studies* (1991). This volume explores the difficulty in transforming the curriculum, the "essentials" in pedagogy and theory for such a transformation, and a black feminist perspective on the academy.

The use of gender as an analytical category is addressed in both *Women's Studies in the South* and *The Impact of Feminist Research in the Academy.* The latter examines methodology in feminist research and the impact of women's studies on particular disciplines. *Women's Studies in the South* (1991), a product of 15 years of experience for students and faculty at the University of Alabama, Tuscaloosa, reviews the development of women's studies and the feminist movement, forms of institutionalized oppression, and the intersection of feminist scholarship and activism. As in African-American studies, the multiple goals for women's studies leave many feminist scholars torn between priorities in research that advance the field; in teaching that transforms individuals; and in advocacy that is often necessary to sustain women's issues, programs, and centers on college and university campuses.

An example of the growth and impact of women's studies internationally is chronicled in *Working Out: New Directions for Women's Studies,* an edited volume of papers from the 1991 Women's Studies Network's (UK) annual conference. Separate chapters are devoted to the politics and practice of women's studies and feminist theory and women's studies in East-Central Europe.

## Disciplines

The impact of multiculturalism at the disciplinary level is reflected in (1) new courses within disciplines that incorporate issues of race/ethnicity, gender, and class and (2) the integration of emerging scholarship into existing courses, often in core requirements. The annotations herein by discipline are largely descriptive and are reported by those who have introduced new courses, modified existing courses, and/or opened new fields of study. Additionally, although limited in number for certain disciplines, the annotations reflect that change is widespread, from law to teacher education to the humanities. According to the traditionalists, few disciplines remain "unscathed." It is likely that all fields have been affected by the emerging scholarship, at some place, at some time, by someone, although the magnitude and impact of change overall in the disciplines still are indeterminate.

At the disciplinary level, two methods are used to effect change in resources: producing curriculum materials and assisting in textbook revisions. Thus, many of the workshops and projects nationwide during the 1980s focused on the production of materials and the introduction of the emerging scholarship in faculty development workshops. In addition to philanthropic support for curriculum integration projects, many of the activities at the disciplinary level may be attributed to national professional societies. In recent years, many disciplinary associations have formed women's subsections or established projects focusing on diversity in the curriculum. An example is the American Anthropological Association's Project on Gender and the Curriculum, which brought together feminist scholarship in cultural anthropology, archeology, primatology, physical anthropology, linguistics, and applied anthropology for use by faculty in introductory and other undergraduate anthropology courses.

The interest in multiculturalism in science and mathematics has been partially fueled by the recognition nationally of the low involvement of women in these disciplines and by the loss of female talent in these areas as girls increasingly withdraw from math and science as they progress in school. Numerous national reports and study commissions have focused on the reasons for this condition and made recommendations for a correction. And as the literature reveals, the reformists view the content of the curriculum and the teaching methodologies associated with math and science as subtly, if not overtly, related to the gender imbalance by perpetuating a sexist and/or racist paradigm that is alienating to women and people of color.

In literature and English much attention has focused on bringing previously neglected works and authors into the canon and on critically analyzing current works for their treatment of issues of race, gender, and class. Perhaps no field has experienced the "wars" as intensely and sustained as those in the humanities, where the "Old Masters" and "Great Books" were literally, or in perspective, Eurocentric, white, and male.

Teacher education reformists not only are involved with multicultural perspectives in the content areas of teacher preparation programs, but also are concerned with the process of teaching and the ultimate holistic impact of teachers on primary and secondary students, their aspirations, achievement, and self-esteem. Annually, nationwide almost 90 percent of education graduates (baccalaureate level) are white, non-Hispanic, and almost three-quarters female. Efforts at reform at the teacher preparation level are aimed at introducing these students to multicultural issues and emphasizing the importance of rolemodeling as it enhances or detracts from the learning environment of future students. Teacher education is, thus, concerned with multicultural education for its importance to the way teachers plan for, evaluate, and ultimately "interact" with diverse groups of students in increasingly heterogeneous classrooms.

Other examples of impact at the discipline level come from communications, psychology, public administration, and religion. Each field shares in common a coming to terms with the rationale for multicultural education, and each discipline deals with the "what" and "how" of multiculturalism in field-specific ways, based on "their" traditional canon, the emerging scholarship, and the impetus for change.

## Traditional Disciplines

*Anthropology*

109.    Kemper, Robert V., and Lawrence B. Breitborde, eds. "Teaching Anthropology: From the Curricular System to the World System." *Urban Anthropology* 18 (1) (Spring 1989):1-151.

Divides this issue into three major categories: (1) *Negotiating the Curricular System* (articles on competing models for the anthropology major, disciplinary and interdisciplinary teaching at Southern Methodist University, the present status and prospects for anthropology at Cleveland State University, and the experience from a small college of the institutional integration of anthropology); (2) *Teaching Anthropology to New Audiences* (articles on international students in the classroom, nonanthropologists who teach the discipline, course selection and content in the absence of program and general-education requirements, and cross-cultural processes for negotiating meaning); and (3) *Interdisciplinary Intellectual Themes* (articles on problems in communication in interdisciplinary education; teaching anthropology in women's studies; anthropology in a value-centered curriculum; world system theory for integrating the social science curriculum; and anthropology, political economy, and the general education curriculum).

110. Morgen, Sandra. "Challenging the Politics of Exclusion: The Perspective of Feminist Anthropology." *Education and Urban Society* 22 (4) (August 1990): 393-401.

Focuses on the charges against feminists in Allan Bloom's *The Closing of the American Mind* and addresses the challenge feminist scholarship in anthropology poses for Bloom and other neoconservatives. Also, presents arguments by William Bennett and Lynne Cheney, who tend to buttress Bloom's politics of exclusion. Offers examples, such as a 1988 report by the Association of American Colleges' Task Force on General Education, that counter those arguments by showing how higher education is actually responding to challenges from a more diversified student body and from the increasing pressure for multicultural curricula. Looks at particular aspects of anthropology that are in the vanguard for change: for example, the specialized area of cultural anthropology with its new research on women and gender and its erosion of the adequacy of traditional approaches to the study of labor, kinship, stratification and the organization of power, and the rise of the state; the growing emphasis on cultural diversity; and the increasing number of feminist perspectives and insights propelled into the discipline by the American Anthropological Association Project on Gender and Curriculum.

111. Morgen, Sandra, and Mary Moran. "Transforming Introductory Anthropology: The American Anthropological Association Project on Gender and the Curriculum." *Women's Studies Quarterly* 18 (1 & 2) (Spring/Summer 1990): 95-104.

Examines the two main methods used by the Association's Project on Gender and the Curriculum to effect change and challenge the prevailing androcentric tradition in anthropology: producing curriculum materials and assisting in textbook revisions. Details the development of a curricular guide, *Gender and Anthropology: Critical Reviews for*

*Research and Teaching,* which brings together feminist scholarship in cultural anthropology, archeology, primatology, physical anthropology, linguistics, and applied anthropology for use by faculty in introductory, and other, undergraduate anthropology courses. Explains and illustrates how this guide combines the feminist critique of dominant theories and understandings with the goal of curricular integration. Examines, also, the project's attempt to revise introductory textbooks by consulting with the authors of at least three of the major textbooks in the field. Comments on (1) the inability to envision the exact changes, given the time lag in textbook publishing, that these efforts will create, and (2) the historically peripheral nature of feminist scholarship. Cautions about the need, therefore, to focus on long-term change(s).

112.    Williams, Charles S. "Teaching Anthropology: Cross-Cultural Processes for Negotiating Meaning." *Urban Anthropology* 18 (1) (Spring 1989): 85-93.

Stresses, initially, the fact that shifting student demographics can allow anthropologists to reexamine some important content dimensions of anthropology, the anthropology curriculum, and the pedagogical strategies to communicate anthropological concepts. Also explores the idea of using increasingly multicultural classrooms as microcommunities that can serve as models for developing interracial and ethnic communication in urban neighborhoods. Advocates and discusses the value of situational learning in introductory courses; the necessity of identifying and critiquing the residual, but persistent, themes of white superiority and colonialism in contemporary texts; the redefinition and expansion of the concept of culture change; and the necessity of creating or rediscovering concepts and themes that are unifying between human cultures. Looks at the use in the classroom of personal narratives as sources of ethnographic detail and, outside the classroom, of field experiences. Surveys a number of texts to analyze lingering ethnocentric themes and emphasizes the imaginative search for the internal logic and coherence in societies beyond one's own.

*Communications*

113.  Carter, Kathryn, and Carol Spitzack. "Transformation and Empowerment in Gender and Communication Courses." *Women's Studies in Communication* 13 (1) (Spring 1990): 92-110.

Discusses the increasing popularity of higher-education courses in gender and communications, which focus on interrelationships among language, social reality, stereotyping, and cultural ideology. Looks at the dynamics of a course on gender and communication that highlights students' responses to core issues taught in three units: acknowledging stereotypes, resistance, and empowerment. Discusses class strategies and methodologies and the growth of students' perceptions. Includes an extensive selected reading list.

114.  Koester, Jolene, and Myron W. Lustig. "Communication Curricula in the Multicultural University." *Communication Education* 40 (July 1991): 250-254.

Argues for communication faculty to construct and revise curricula that will respond to an increasingly multicultural student body. Examines the present undergraduate curriculum in communication, which operates on a rather culturally narrow foundation, and suggests that instructors of communication should examine the content of their courses and determine to what degree the content reflects a set of assumptions and a point of view that may be appropriate only for students from a limited number of cultures. Gives five suggestions for developing communication curricula appropriate to a multicultural university. Asserts that theory development must be generalizable beyond the United States' Anglo population.

115.    Mandziuk, Roseann M., ed. "Special Symposium —
        Revisioning the Curriculum." *Women's Studies in
        Communication* 15 (2) (Fall 1992): 51-96.

        Along with two other articles, offers three essays that
        originated as a program at the 1991 annual meeting of the
        Speech Communication Association in Atlanta, Georgia.
        Presents the authors' efforts to revise three of the most
        entrenched areas in communication: causes in public
        speaking, public address, and argumentation. Notes the
        influence on the revisions, not only of feminist scholarship
        but also of Afrocentric and other alternate perspectives.
        Includes specific course components for each area, as well as
        useful resource material. Also includes by one of the original
        set reviewers a concluding summary commentary.

116.    Powell, Robert, and Mary Jane Collier. "Public Speaking
        Instruction and Cultural Bias: The Future of the Basic
        Course." *American Behavioral Scientist* 34 (2)
        (November/December 1990): 240-250.

        Looks at the background of basic oral-communication
        courses and their tendency primarily to emphasize public
        speaking skills. Raises questions about the changing cultural
        composition of the student body and the shifts in
        communication demands these students will face in the
        future. Analyzes three main limitations that continue to
        militate against oral-communication courses becoming more
        multiculturally sensitive and responsive: instruction in
        public speaking is culturally ethnocentric, opportunities for
        success in multicultural public speaking classes are unequal,
        and traditional public speaking courses do not encourage
        competencies that generalize to a variety of communication
        settings. Assesses some of the most salient factors and
        contexts that argue strongly for fundamental curricular
        changes that will help to meet the challenges that lie ahead
        for students outside of the academy.

*Fine Arts*

117.  Collins, Georgia, and Renee Sandell. "The Politics of Multicultural Art Education." *Art Education* 45 (6) (November 1992): 8-13.

Notes the effect of multiculturalism on art and art education and analyzes the tendencies of four particular responses within cultural pluralism that need further critique: (1) the attack response, which denigrates Western mainstream art but accepts other cultures; art without critical examination; (2) the escape response, which encourages diversity for its own sake, romanticizes the exotic, and ignores the unpleasant or problematic; (3) the repair response, which implies that positive acceptance of other cultures' art can build positive self-concepts; and (4) the transformative response, which envisions art as a central player in helping to create a more serene, common culture that, at the same time, tolerates separate cultural differences. Argues, ultimately, for a pluralist approach characterized by the best of both integrationist and separatist orientations.

118.  Klocko, David G. "Multicultural Music in the College Curriculum." *Music Educators [sic] Journal* 75 (5) (January 1989): 38-41.

Describes the lack of a global perspective in current university curricula and calls for the study of music literature, specifically, to include folk, popular, and classical music of Europe and North America as well as other cultures. Describes the current unacceptable music-major course sequence that.is largely limited to the European classical tradition and that, therefore, ignores and devalues both other international music and the previous music experiences of the students themselves. Argues against the notion that the traditional Western classical music heritage will suffer because of a more globally inclusive, comprehensive curriculum. Presents musicological and practical rationales for curricular expansion, looks at some previous efforts to change, and discusses some more ideal course offerings and sequences. Also discusses graduate curricula and faculty potential inside a more comprehensive curriculum.

119.    McClary, Susan. "Reshaping a Discipline: Musicology and Feminism in the 1990s." *Feminist Studies* 19 (2) (Summer 1993): 399-423.

Reports that research on women in music began to appear in the 1970s and finds that feminist musicology generates less controversy than feminist music criticism. Briefly reviews research on women in music history, noting the rediscovery and discovery of women musicians from earlier centuries. Discusses texts and resources in feminist musicology useful for new courses or in revising existing courses. Discusses feminists' interests in popular music and world music. Explores the difficulties in, emergence of, and objections to feminist music criticism; also cites research, activities, and texts in this area. Concludes that feminism has permanently transformed musicology.

120.    Portuges, Catherine. "The Spectacle of Gender: Cinema and Psyche." In *Gendered Subjects: The Dynamics of Feminist Teaching,* edited by Margaret Culley and Catherine Portuges, 183-194. Boston, MA: Routledge & Kegan Paul, 1985.

Puts into perspective the inherent problems for the psychoanalytically oriented feminist teacher of film: students' general desire not to analyze films, not to be predisposed to psychoanalytic theory, and not readily accepting of the persistent questions of gender. Then presents the social, historical, and theoretical rationales for teaching a class on cinema from such a controversial — or at least contentious — set of perspectives. Examines some of the interdisciplinary methodology that must be incorporated and some of the texts and films and how they fit into her class dynamics. Draws parallels between films and their respective sociohistorical contexts. Discusses a specific course, *French Women Since The Second Sex,* and the use of traditional texts used for feminist purposes. Discusses, also, the impact of this interactive course on her, as well as on her students.

*History*

121.    Butler, Johnnella E., and Betty Schmitz. "Different Voices: A Model Institute for Integrating Women of Color into Undergraduate American Literature and History Courses." In *Transforming the Curriculum: Ethnic Studies and Women's Studies,* edited by Johnnella E. Butler and John C. Walter, 51-61. Albany, NY: State University of New York Press, 1991.

Presents the most salient results of The Different Voices Institute, funded by the Ford Foundation and sponsored as a week-long residential experience at the University of Washington's Northwest Center for Research on Women. Explains that the Institute was aimed at providing participants with theoretical frameworks, illustrative readings, and pedagogical strategies that can be used to incorporate women of color into undergraduate American history and literature courses. Also notes the problem of women's studies use of gender as the main dimension in analyzing and describing the experiences of women. Calls for specific changes to counteract this bias and offers a number of strategies for course revision and general curricular transformation. Presents new approaches to syllabi construction.

122.    Hurwitz, Ellen S. "Teaching About Men and Women in History: Experimenting in Curricular Reform." *Liberal Education* 67 (3) (Fall 1981): 205-208.

Looks at the development of a course on the history of Russia and the U.S.S.R. which attempts to correct the textbook and primary sources used in the course with data about Russian and Soviet women. Lafayette College opened its doors to female students in 1970. Focuses on the present (1981) attempt to go beyond gender dichotomies and to integrate new knowledge and scholarship on women into the existing, male-oriented histories available. Presents strategies and assesses the value of this integrative approach over a more radical feminist approach to historical revision.

123.    Leonard, Virginia W. "Integrating Women's History into the Secondary and College Curriculum." *The Social Studies* 72 (6) (November/December 1981): 265-270.

Presents some of the particular problems related to integrating women's history into the curriculum, as opposed to establishing separate courses on women. Analyzes the ways in which women's history has begun to challenge and change at least three of the basic theoretical bases and assumptions that undergird the traditional concept(s) of an androcentric, Eurocentric approach to understanding history. Then presents four possible approaches to incorporating women's history materials into existing classes — biographical, political, historical era, and family/community history — and an extensive list of materials that can be useful for each of these.

124.    Mullaney, Marie Marmo. "'From Plato to Pareto': The Western Civilization Course Reconsidered." *The Journal of General Education* 38 (1) (1986): 28-40.

Largely defends the traditional approach to teaching *Western Civilization*, the standard freshman survey in history. Notes the developmental history of the course itself, focusing on rationale, inherent validity, and social and cultural processes that have forced changes. Defends the general-education ideal of the centrality of the traditional course, but does admit the necessity of inclusion within that basic, accepted framework of the broadest range of peoples and events. Argues for a course that is chronologically grounded, concept-based, and issue-oriented that maintains its European/American focus and integrates the experiences of others.

125.    Stearns, Peter. "Linking Humanities Research and Teaching." *Liberal Education* 77 (3) (May/June 1991): 22-27.

Analyzes some of the philosophical and pragmatic differences among current humanities studies and curricula and presents some of the integrative themes that cross disciplinary lines. Using history as a specific example, defends the need to reevaluate previous teaching staples so that the new social history of the less powerful and articulate are included in current dialogue. Examines some of the problems inherent in such a curricular and pedagogical expansion (e.g., lack of coordination between staid curricula and new research), and the basic difficulty in changing a traditional, entrenched canon. Assesses some of the attacks on the fixed canon, looking at the positive and negative aspects of this criticism. Then outlines a new integrative approach that attempts to incorporate the best of both the fixed canon and the valid contemporary criticism. Presents a translation of this approach into a hypothetical curriculum that includes the core program itself and, even, the possibility for a new integrated major for students with cross-disciplinary interests. Emphasizes coherence and the necessity to accommodate the differences between innovation and convention.

*Law*

126.    Rifkin, Janet. "Teaching Mediation: A Feminist Perspective on the Study of Law." In *Gendered Subjects: The Dynamics of Feminist Teaching*, edited by Margaret Culley and Catherine Portuges, 96-107. Boston, MA: Routledge & Kegan Paul, 1985.

Introduces alternative approaches both to understanding the basics of one legal system and to teaching classes to law students. Examines how the traditional, formal legal system offers limited possibilities for conflict resolution and shows how the adversarial system clearly heightens the underlying dispute. Discusses as background, the teaching of a course, Women and the Law, which presents law as a symbol and vehicle of male authority and leads to the emphasis on mediation rather than adversarial confrontation as a viable option for resolving social conflict in general, and women's issues specifically. Presents a theory and critique of mediation and an analysis of the structure and impact of a later class (Alternatives to the Adversary Process) that challenges aspects of the traditional authority structures and gender hierarchy in society. Compares resolution by mediation with resolution by adjudication and assesses the former's emphasis on discussion, compromise, and consensus when assisted by third-party neutrals. Discusses also the moral dimension of mediation discussion and the need to understand the relationship between patriarchal power and the law.

*Literature/English*

127.    Demaray, Elyse, and Lori Landay. "Senses of Self: Women Writers of the Harlem Renaissance." *Feminist Teacher* 5 (2) (Fall 1990): 32-33.

        Describes a course designed for undergraduate sophomores and juniors that explores the writings of women of the Harlem Renaissance and raises the important issue of canon formation, as well as those of race, class, and gender. Notes a number of specific qualities of the course that distinguish it from those courses that usually focus on the more traditional literature of the black male: questions about how literary movements are defined; differences in issues addressed by male and female authors; pitfalls in generalizing about gender experiences; the stereotype of the black woman; and ways in which race, class, and gender influence definitions of identity. Includes the class syllabus and a bibliography.

128.    Hairston, Maxine. "Diversity, Ideology, and Teaching Writing." *College Composition and Communication* 43 (2) (May 1992): 179-193.

        Criticizes what she sees as the emerging model for freshman writing programs, putting dogma, politics, ideology, and social goals of faculty before student's educational needs. Offers numerous teachers' quotes to illustrate this trend and presents an analysis of two major social forces outside the liberal arts that are contributing to creating an environment conducive to the new model: the tremendous increase in diversity in the student population and the response of many intellectuals to the conservative, right-wing forces dominate in American politics over the past decade. Argues for a more-thoughtful, better-balanced use of multicultural concepts and diversity in a classroom emphasized by solid intellectual and writing goals, not ideological or political ones.

129.   Jay, Gregory S. "The End of 'American' Literature: Toward a Multicultural Practice." *College English* 53 (3) (March 1991): 264-281.

Argues philosophically and experientially for a radical, fundamental curricular change. Insists that American literature must be discontinued in its present state, not just revised, and that a new conceptual model must be envisioned. Defends, also, the need to construct a multicultural and dialogical paradigm for the study of writing in the United States. Rejects the melting pot notion of American culture and offers a rationale for curricular change based, rather, on the assumption that multicultural interdependence takes precedence over any myth of assimilation. Advances that the myth is as great and pernicious in literary history as it is in social and political history. Proposes and describes a new course, *Writing in the United States*, a course with a geographical and historical paradigm (another possible course title is *Comparative American Literature*). Describes related experiences teaching African-American and Jewish-American literature and defends the need to move beyond traditional, classic themes of American literature (e.g., *the Virgin Land, the Frontier West, Innocence versus Experience*).

130.   Jenkins, Ruth Y. "The Intersection of Gender and Culture in the Teaching of Writing." *College Teaching* 41 (1) (Winter 1993): 19-24.

Begins by discussing the changing academy and then moves to question what to assign, how to teach, and how to assess in the teaching of writing. Discusses feminist theory and the relationship to traditional argument (or Aristotelian discourse), the preferred rhetorical/organizational model in the university. Argues that the cultural context of effective writing should be a major focus of concern. Cautions against identifying difference as error in organizational and rhetorical patterns. Cites the limitations placed on students and the corresponding discouragement many students experience in being evaluated solely against traditional argument. Notes the quick recognition that academics give to variety in writing across fields while being blind to variety within disciplines. Calls on faculty to broaden their understanding of writing and accept the fallibility of the universal superiority of Eurocentric modes of style and thought.

131.   Lauter, Paul. "Reconstructing American Literature: A Strategy for Change." In *Toward a Balanced Curriculum: A Sourcebook for Initiating Gender Integration Projects*, edited by Bonnie B. Spanier, Alexander Bloom, and Darlene Boroviak, 142-154. Cambridge, MA: Schenkman Publishing Company, Inc., 1984.

Discusses the necessary dialectic between change-oriented projects based on a single campus and covering many disciplines, and those focused on one discipline, in this case, American literature. Argues for a greater inclusiveness by the addition of more works by women and minorities without sacrificing intellectual, academic credibility or canon quality. Notes that a personal 1981 survey of over 500 course syllabi at selected colleges and universities yielded results that represent no significant improvement over the results of a 1948 National Council of Teachers of English survey. Pinpoints and analyzes the most critical tool that is necessary to accomplish such a change, the anthologies used in American literature courses. Assesses some of the economic and organizational barriers to change in the publishing industry and some of the efforts being made to hurdle these barriers.

132.    Marks, Elaine. "Deconstructing in Women's Studies to Reconstructing the Humanities." In *Women's Place in the Academy: Transforming the Liberal Arts Curriculum*, edited by Marilyn R. Schuster and Susan R. Van Dyne, 172-187. Totowa, NJ: Rowman and Allanheld, 1985.

Describes the intersections between feminist and post-structuralist theorizing by a teacher of French literature and of comparative U.S. and French feminist theory and practice. Explores the theoretical and the disciplinary similarities of women's studies and French post-structuralism and the ways by which both radically can revise paradigms, not just add more information to an existing corpus of knowledge. Illustrates how a women's studies curriculum deconstructs traditional humanities courses by describing a University of Wisconsin introductory humanities core course, *Meanings of Women in Western Culture*, and a French department course, *French Women Writers Today*. Explains the fundamental differences between these courses and more traditional ones. Describes how such new courses and such disciplinary intersections can provide theoretical guidelines and pedagogical practice that transform the traditional curriculum.

133.    Ruszkiewics, John. "'Reason is but Choosing': Ideology in First-Year English." Paper presented at the annual meeting of the Conference on College Composition and Communication, Boston, 21-23 March 1991. ERIC, ED 331058.

Critiques the controversial first-year writing course at the University of Texas, Austin. Laments, especially, the overly political nature of courses such as the Texas one that incorporate the tenets of critical literacy at the expense of composition fundamentals. Discusses the problems of such a curricular shift and offers recommendations for avoiding the negative results of Texas's *difference* curriculum; for example, creating the program more slowly and systematically, soliciting the opinions of valid constituencies who disagree, recognizing that ideology is challengeable, and accommodating a variety of pedagogical approaches into a multicultural syllabus.

134.    Schilb, John. "Transforming a Course in American Literary Realism." In *Women's Place in the Academy: Transforming the Liberal Arts Curriculum*, edited by Marilyn R. Schuster and Susan R. Van Dyne, 201-220. Totowa, NJ: Rowman and Allanheld, 1985.

Examines the transformation of the course, American Realism, in the English department at the University of North Carolina-Wilmington, from a course defined by a narrow canon occupied almost exclusively by white male writers to one defined by the larger inclusion of both women and blacks. Delineates the process of rethinking the syllabus and questioning the canon, yet, at the same time, dealing with unavoidable anxiety that accompanies challenging the canon. Explains how the obstacles and the anxiety led to an understanding — but not an endorsement — of colleagues' similar feelings and reticence about change. Presents a theoretical and programmatic rationale for the decision to alter class content and orientation and the need to redefine realism and reconceive gender. Discusses the intellectual rigor that must, and can, be maintained by such a transformation. Defends the rightness, the wisdom, and the enactment of a more-expansive inclusion. Offers specific-course objectives, required readings, and required writing.

135.    Showalter, Elaine, ed. *The New Feminist Criticism: Essays on Women, Literature, and Theory*. New York: Pantheon Books, 1985. 403 pp.

Explores in three major sections the growing impact of developing feminist theory on the academy, especially concerning, for example, poetics, criticism, and literature: (1) the effects of feminist critics on both the canon and the overall academy (e.g., injecting new spirit into English studies, gender and the interpretation of literary texts, exclusionary theories of American fiction, and feminist challenges to the canon), (2) feminist criticisms and women's cultures (e.g., feminist poetic, feminist literary criticism, black feminist criticism, and lesbian feminist criticism), and (3) feminist critical theories related specifically to women's writing (e.g., issues of female creativity, women poets, and an overall understanding of French discussions of feminist writings). Also includes an extensive topical bibliography, as well as a list of journals publishing feminist criticism.

## Mathematics and Science

136. Anderson, S.E. "Worldmath Curriculum: Fighting Eurocentrism in Mathematics." *Journal of Negro Education* 59 (3) (1990): 348-359.

Explores how mathematics can be taught without what some would perceive as a racist and sexist Eurocentric bias. Discusses the four historiographic pillars underlying the present structure of mathematics education and research and presents six major pedagogical mistakes in mathematics teaching: (1) separating arithmetic from algebra; (2) teaching math without historical references; (3) using elitist and cryptic textbooks; (4) emphasizing individual rather than cooperative learning; (5) accepting the myth that math is pure abstraction and antithetical to one's cultural environment; and (6) overemphasizing memorization. Argues that it is imperative to include the contributions, especially in a historical context, of African, Indian, Chinese, and Mayan mathematics and mathematicians. Offers an alternative curriculum and pedagogy and details the structure and dynamics of an algebra class comprised principally of working-class black and Latino adults and taught from a more holistic, alternative approach.

137. Ayers-Nachamkin, Beverly. "A Feminist Approach to the Introductory Statistics Course." *Women's Studies Quarterly* 20 (1 & 2) (Spring/Summer 1992): 86-94.

Describes a course initiated at a small liberal arts college for women. Discusses the prevalence of math anxiety for many women and the need to (1) de-emphasize the authority position of the professor and (2) increase cooperative learning while reducing competitiveness. Places the course's emphasis always on process rather than on product and precise answers. Presents the pedagogical techniques, philosophical rationales, choice of examples, and testing procedures that defined class dynamics. Includes references and an edited version of the author's *Math Anxiety Bill of Rights (and responsibilities)*.

138.    Breene, L. Anne. "Women and Computer Science." *Initiatives* 55 (2) (1993): 39-44.

Documents some of the continuing hostility to women in computer science, as well as the difficulty in recruiting and retaining women faculty in computer science departments. Discusses sex bias in the curriculum and issues concerning women in computer science education and the workplace. Notes, specifically, such problems as confusion in computer classrooms at the middle school and secondary levels, the lack of a standard public school curriculum, sex-biased educational software, dominance of males in computer labs, the large number of non-American university professors who exhibit cultural biases against women, and the biases inherent in key operational definitions. Offers personal comments and extensive references.

139.    Cayleff, Susan E. "Teaching Women's History in a Medical School: Challenges and Possibilities." *Women's Studies Quarterly* 16 (1 & 2) (Spring/Summer 1988): 97-109.

Charts the experience of a current associate professor of women's studies who previously taught women's history to six distinct constituencies of nurse specialists at the University of Texas Medical Branch in Galveston. Focuses on classes taught to three of these groups: first-year medical students, obstetrics and gynecology residents and faculty, and nurse practitioners already having a B.S. in nursing.

Examines some of the difficulty in teaching aspects of theoretical feminist scholarship to students with such purely scientific backgrounds. Presents the nature of classes taught to these three specific groups and the strategies that worked most effectively. Comments on the general receptivity of health-care workers to these ideas and the ways in which examining the historical precedents of gender, power, and healing can lead to a more profound understanding of both the ethical dimension of their profession and the ways in which such knowledge can be empowering.

140. Farrant, Patricia A., and Alice Miller, eds. "Gender Equity in Math and Science, Part 1." *Initiatives* 55 (2) (1993): 65.

Includes articles on removing barriers for undergraduate women in the sciences, improving science by increasing diversity among scientists, examining a program to retain students in science and math-related majors, empowering women in math, assessing the status of women in computer science, cultivating scientists at women's colleges, analyzing the role of community and collaboration for assisting women and minorities in science, and looking at the activities and growth of women engineers.

141. Farrant, Patricia A., and Alice Miller, eds. "Gender Equity in Math and Science, Part 2." *Initiatives* 55 (3) (1993): 71.

Offers essays that describe how to narrow the gap between the success of males and females in mathematics and science. Includes essays on a mentoring program to assist retention of women science students; an examination of the causes of female underrepresentation in engineering and physical sciences; the key to successful intervention programs; activities to enhance minority-female readiness, recruitment, and retention in the sciences; a women-in-science project at Dartmouth; the success of a summer mathematics program at Mount Holyoke College; successful strategies in Purdue's attempts to increase the participation of women in engineering; and the need to alter or reform science-teacher education to help ensure female success in K-12 science classes.

142.     Fausto-Sterling, Anne, and Lydia L. English. *Women and Minorities in Science: An Interdisciplinary Course,* Working Paper no. 154. Wellesley, MA: Wellesley College, Center for Research on Women, 1985. ERIC, ED 281752.

Presents a description of a course entitled, Women and Minorities in Science, developed to bridge the gap between Afro-American studies and traditional women's studies courses. Provides a description of how the course was developed and discusses content and instructional approach. Also includes basic course description — with instructor analysis and commentary — and a list of resource materials, sources, and reference works.

143.     Jackson, Allyn. "Multiculturalism in Mathematics: Historical Truth or Political Correctness?" In *Heeding the Call for Change: Suggestions for Curricular Action,* edited by Lynn Arthur Steen, 121-134. Washington, DC: The Mathematical Association of America, 1992.

Acknowledges both the multiculturalism vs. political-correctness debate and the apparently growing interest in a multicultural perspective on mathematics, a discipline that many feel is inherently objective, neutral, and independent of culture. Describes the growing prominence of (1) ethnomathematics, which analyzes mathematical ideas in their historical, cultural, political, and social contexts, and (2) humanistic mathematics, which focuses on the role of intuition, discovery, emotions, and values in mathematical development. Explores the seminal question that such new perspectives raise: whether math is culturally independent or environmentally influenced (or, implicitly, both). Examines some of the major developing arguments by, for example, women, blacks, and Muslims. Analyzes the charge that traditional math is Eurocentric with Western concepts as the ultimate yardstick by which all other contributions are measured. Presents four institutions (Middlebury College,

Ithaca College, Harvey Mudd College, and Clark Atlanta University) that have incorporated elements of multiculturalism into their math curricula. Finally, examines some of the major critics of multicultural approaches. Includes a list of readings related to multiculturalism, ethnomathematics, and non-Eurocentric contributions to the discipline.

144.     Presmeg, Norma C. "School Mathematics in Culture-Conflict Situations." *Educational Studies in Mathematics* 19 (2) (May 1988): 163-177.

Examines the ways in which an institution — in this case, the University of Durban-Westville (Durban's South Africa) — can restructure a mathematics curriculum that is responsive to multicultural needs, especially following a period of cultural change. Presents a demographic look at the university and some of the immediate historical background, characterized by boycotts and other disruptions that took many students away from classes, interrupted teaching and learning schedules, and signaled the imperatives of a changing social order. Details with specific examples some of the problems and successes attendant when representatives of many cultures try to design a mathematics curriculum and to contribute to promoting understanding and tolerance. Examines the acculturation problems of many students, along with the concomitant changing views of what should constitute a viable curriculum in such a dynamic and uncertain time. Assesses the need to change both methods and content, yet still ensure student mastery of that which is fundamentally consistent, useful, and necessary in mathematical comprehension. Focuses on the need, also, to adapt to the actual class makeup.

145.     Rogers, Pat, and Gabriele Kaiser, eds. *Equity in Mathematics Education: Influences of Feminism and Culture.* London: The Falmer Press, 1995. 278 pp.

Using four broad categories — effecting change, the cultural context, feminist pedagogy in mathematics education, and changing the discipline — provides an overview of developments in the field of gender and mathematics education. Organizes the book around Peggy McIntosh's typology (1983) of five phases of curricular revision to examine change: (1) womanless mathematics, (2) women in mathematics, (3) women as a problem in mathematics, (4) women as central to mathematics, and (5) mathematics reconstructed. Views mathematics as being between phases three and four. Largely uses cases and examples from school mathematics. Clearly, however, explores the impact of feminism on the discipline in several chapters on feminist pedagogy. Presents perspectives from researchers around the globe, including cultural experiences from Singapore, New Guinea, France, and Malawi.

146.    Rosser, Sue V. "Integrating the Feminist Perspective into Courses in Introductory Biology." In *Women's Place in the Academy: Transforming the Liberal Arts Curriculum*, edited by Marilyn R. Schuster and Susan R. Van Dyne, 258-276. Totowa, NJ: Rowman and Allanheld, 1985.

Proposes that the feminist perspective developed in recent years reveals that what seems to be objective research in the sciences actually reflects a masculine point of view. Presents various critiques of science by feminists and analyzes the tendency to equate an androcentric perspective with objectivity. Then takes the five broad fields within biology — the cell, genetics, development, evolution, and ecology — as well as the traditional scientific method, and under each, details how an introductory biology course might be structured to include a feminist perspective. Looks at how a more-inclusive perspective can lead to differences in model selection, experimental subjects, and data interpretations. Shows how enriched theories may be compared to traditional, unicausal theories. Offers an extensive list of additional readings and a syllabus for a specific course, *Contemporary General Biology*.

147.    Shahn, Ezra. "Science as Another Culture/Science as a Part of Culture." *American Behavioral Scientist* 34 (2) (November/December 1990): 210-222.

Based on the premise that there are no inherent or culturally based impediments to learning science, considers how to offer science in a meaningful way to a multicultural population. Examines a number of approaches to teaching that acknowledge student differences and discusses a specific course, *Foundations of Science*. Describes a one-year, multidisciplinary course with laboratory exercises developed specifically for nonscience majors. Presents, first, an overview of science as a social construct, not as the basis of any unique culture but as a part of any culture. Looks at a number of disparate cultures across both space and time to validate this concept and to solidify the notion that specific culture in any way is an inherently limiting factor in understanding and applying scientific knowledge. Emphasizes the core of the class, which shows that scientific concepts are developed from new information, new technology, and/or changing philosophical or societal limitations. Uses a basically narrative, historical approach that provides insight into the reasons a particular developmental story is followed. Assesses the course's success and its implications for the use of a similar thematic model in which breadth is sacrificed for conceptual depth.

*Psychology*

148.    Brown, Pearl L., and Michele Hoffnung. "Images of Women in Psychology and Literature: An Interdisciplinary Course." *Feminist Teacher* 6 (1) (Summer 1991): 14-20.

Describes the revision of a junior-senior-level interdisciplinary course in psychology and literature at a small, private, liberal arts college. Notes that the revision tries to balance the theoretical and philosophical concerns of both disciplines and provides an introduction to recent feminist theory in both psychology and literature. Presents three main objectives: the inclusion of recent research in the psychology of women, an introduction of contemporary feminist literary theory as a response to traditional theories, and the provision of a perspective on the impact of the ideology of western culture on the lives of women. Describes the selection of topics and gives an extensive explanation of course construction and divisions. Includes a sample syllabus and a list of both required texts and supplementary reserve materials.

149.    Kroll, Judith F., Francine M. Deutsch, and Kathleen McAuley. "Becoming Scientists: Integrating Women into the Psychology Curriculum at Mount Holyoke." *Initiatives* 53 (4) (Winter 1991): 25-33.

Describes the attempt by Mount Holyoke faculty to encourage women students in psychology to think about themselves as potential scientists. Describes a program of curricular change based on the belief that it is essential for women students to have access to information about the lives and work of women that goes beyond the appearance of women scientists in the classroom. Explains, specifically, the required *Experimental Methods* course and the three exercises that were implemented to effect positive change: the students write about their own lives; they read about the history of women in science; and they hear about the lives and work of contemporary psychologists from those in the field. Details how each of these exercises was integrated into the course, which still maintained the traditional research-methods curriculum. Presents a summative analysis and list of references.

150.    Porter, Nancy, ed. "Feminist Psychology: Curriculum and Pedagogy." *Women's Studies Quarterly* 20 (1 & 2) (Spring/Summer 1992): 7-115.

Includes articles on psychology's paradigm and curricular reconstruction, the relationship between developmental psychology and feminism, identity development issues in a course on Asian-American women, the inclusion of *The Women of Psychology* in psychology courses, research issues on women of color, a feminist approach to the introductory statistics course, the importance of process in developing feminist strategies for teaching about oppression, and the diffusion of linguistic dichotomies.

151. Tatum, Beverly Daniel. "Talking about Race, Learning about Racism: The Application of Racial Identity Development Theory in the Classroom." *Harvard Educational Review* 62 (1) (Spring 1992): 1-24.

Describes the positive impact of a Psychology of Racism course in multicultural classes at three different institutions. Discusses the significance of this formal structure as a vehicle for sharing ideas about racism, ethnic bigotry, etc. Describes, also, the application of racial identity development theory. Identifies three primary sources of student resistance to talking about race and learning about racism. Also covers some strategies for overcoming this resistance. Addresses the institutional implications for such a class and such a use of the racial identity development theory. Emphasizes strongly the need for continual dialogue if we are to have successful multiracial campuses.

152. Wilkinson, Sue. "Why Psychology (Badly) Needs Feminism." In *Out of the Margins: Women's Studies in the Nineties*, edited by Jane Aaron & Sylvia Walby, 191-203. London: The Falmer Press, 1991.

Notes that psychology is the fourth most popular subject of study in Britain with over 75 percent of first-year enrollments by female students; yet as a discipline has resisted feminist influence. Notes the exclusion of women from positions of power in the academy, the invisibility of women in psychological research, the comparison of women to male norms, and the prevailing research traditions that effectively marginalize feminist issues and scholarship. Looks at the current status of the discipline, recent feminist interventions in psychology, and the discipline's resistance. In conclusion, questions the compatibility of psychology and feminism.

*Public Administration*

153.    Burnier, DeLysa. "Administrative Woman and
        Administrative Man: Teaching Public Administration from
        a Gender Inclusive Perspective." *Feminist Teacher* 7 (1) (Fall
        1992): 26-30.

        Details the development of a revised *Principles of Public
        Administration*, a core course in the undergraduate political
        science curriculum at Ohio University (OU). Explains how
        the course was one of a number changed as the result of the
        OU Women's Studies project *Integrating Gender Scholarship:
        Toward An Inclusive Curriculum*. Initiated to introduce gender
        into mainstream courses so that over time courses across the
        curriculum would contain women's issues and scholarship.
        Describes the goals of the revised course as (1) showing that
        women are a significant number in the workforce but that
        workplace equality remains elusive, and (2) acquainting
        students with a range of workplace issues as those relate to
        women, such as affirmative action, leadership, and
        communication differences. Describes textbooks, course
        divisions, student reception, problems, and possible future
        revisions. Includes references and a topic syllabus.

*Religion/Philosophy*

154.    Hagen, June Steffensen, ed. *Gender Matters: Women's Studies
        for the Christian Community*. Grand Rapids, MI: Academic
        Books, 1990. 304 pp.

        Divides its nine chapters into three general areas: (1)
        religion (e.g., theology and feminism and perspectives from
        biblical studies), (2) literature and the arts (i.e., feminist
        reading in literary criticism and the novel and, also, a
        Christian perspective on poetry, music, and art history), and
        (3) the social sciences (i.e., women and the American part;
        gender, society, and church; and the recognition of
        oppression). Offers for each chapter a study guide that
        includes discussion questions, writing suggestions, research

topics, and reading lists. Also includes a scripture index, along with the general index.

155.    Longino, Helen E. "Rethinking Philosophy." In *Women's Place in the Academy: Transforming the Liberal Arts Curriculum*, edited by Marilyn R. Schuster and Susan R. Van Dyne, 188-200. Totowa, NJ: Rowman and Allanheld, 1985.

Uses a description of a single course, *Introduction to Philosophy*, taught at a women's college, to illustrate the need to radically transform the disciplines's androcentric, traditional orientation. Describes how the study of philosophy in the context of a liberal education is intellectual empowerment and how this course went beyond the *Great Books* approach (e.g., Plato, Aristotle, Descartes, Berkeley, and Russell) to one organized around questions relating to the nature of self. Discusses the new anthology used and the challenge of imbuing students with a greater sense of balance and a more clear recognition of conflict within this expanded canon. Analyzes the main challenge that such a nontraditional approach tries to remedy: providing an education that values students' strengths and prepares them to use those in their future lives, and an education that includes them and their interests in an understanding of human life.

156.    Plaskow, Judith. "We Are Also Your Sisters: The Development of Women's Studies in Religion." *Women's Studies Quarterly* 21 (1 & 2) (Spring/Summer 1993): 9-21.

Explores the stepsister status often experienced by women's studies in religion. Discusses the transition from the analysis and critique of male texts, institutions, and traditions to the recovering of women's religion history and, recently, to an emphasis on the transformation of existing traditions and the development of new ones. Purports that feminist studies in religion not only add information to existing knowledge but also challenge basic paradigms. Discusses the strength the field derives from connections to religious communities of women. Asserts that some areas of feminist studies have lost the grassroots connection as they delve increasingly into professional activities and abstract theories. Notes the use by women of color in the field of *womanist* rather than *feminist* because the former signifies conceptions of difference and the term is understood by black church women. Also, briefly touches on the implications for teaching in this often intensely personal sphere and on the importance of these studies to those in undergraduate and graduate programs in seminaries.

## Sociology/Social Science

157.   Abbott, Pamela. "Feminist Perspectives in Sociology: The Challenge to 'Mainstream' Orthodoxy." In *Out of the Margins: Women's Studies in the Nineties*, edited by Jane Aaron & Sylvia Walby, 181-190. London: The Falmer Press, 1991.

Argues from a British perspective that feminist contributions to sociology, both in quantity and quality, are substantial, yet feminist perspectives remain marginal to the discipline. States that research still has a tendency to generalize from male samples and women are textbook chapter add-ons. Notes that reforms in sociology take one of three approaches: integration, separatism, or reconceptualization. Discusses the need to reconceptualize sociology, not just to integrate women into the field. Discusses problems with *malestream* class theory, social mobility research, and the lack of gender focus. Concludes that resistance to feminist ideas in sociology is maintained by the disproportionate number of males in the academy who hold intellectual and institutional power.

158.   Carter, Carolyn, and others. "Integrating Women's Issues in the Social Work Curriculum: A Proposal." *Journal of Social Work Education* 30 (2) (Spring/Summer 1994): 200-216.

Chronicles the development of curricular revisions in the School of Social Work at Arizona State University. Provides examples of course objectives, unit objectives, and suggested readings that integrate women's issues into required MSW courses. Advances that integration of women's issues can only be achieved through the development of new paradigms that include women's experiences. Briefly reviews course changes in direct practice, family practice, human behavior in the social environment, community organization, administration, social welfare, and research methods. Proposes an approach centered in social work values combined with ecological and critical perspectives.

159.   Harvey, Patricia. "Some Reasonable Goals for Sex and Gender Roles Courses." *Teaching Sociology* 14 (July 1986): 181-184.

Gives a brief background of the course, *Sociology of Sex Roles*, at Colorado State University. Details the course's growth and popularity, evidenced by the doubling of male enrollment since 1980 (about 60 percent female and 40 percent male in 1986). Presents a detailed list of course objectives (e.g., ability to list and contrast sociological role theory with theoretical alternatives, such as biological, anthropological, historical, and psychological; knowledge of the forces of socialization; and evaluation of the links between sex roles and the different experiences of men and women in arenas such as art, sports, law, and politics). Also gives some specific tactics used to achieve these objectives. Emphasizes the sharing of ideas and downplays politics. Recommends a number of specific resources, including books, journals, and films, and includes texts that have been successful.

160.   Lewis, Magda. "Interrupting Patriarchy: Politics, Resistance, and Transformation in the Feminist Classroom." *Harvard Educational Review* 60 (4) (November 1990): 467-487.

Examines the rationale, pedagogy, and implications of a sociology-of-education course, *Seminar in Social Class, Gender and Race in Education*, taught at Queen's University, Ontario, Canada. Explains the basic course proposal to develop a critical understanding of the implications of social class, sex/gender differences, and racial background for children's educational experiences. Also investigates the psychological, social, and sexual dynamics of the feminist classroom as the women and men students struggle with the realities of violence against women and the negotiation strategies women use to survive, and even succeed, in a patriarchal society. Analyzes students' resistance and shares some of the teaching strategies used to modify the typical gendered status quo of classroom interaction. Suggests a particular theoretical framework of feminist teaching and the need to make sense of classroom dynamics that often divide women and men and tend to perpetuate women's subordination, both intellectually and physically.

161.    Salem, Greta, and Stephen Sharkey. "Transforming the Social Sciences." In *Women's Place in the Academy: Transforming the Liberal Arts Curriculum*, edited by Marilyn R. Schuster and Susan R. Van Dyne, 231-257. Totowa, NJ: Rowman and Allanheld, 1985.

Describes attempts at Alverno College to transform the teaching of social science by introducing feminist research and practice into the total curriculum. Examines the interdisciplinary program that integrates material mainly from sociology and political science. Pays careful attention to the fundamental concept of empowerment, especially by countering the traditional bias that defines politics as a non-feminine vocation. Explains how the differential effects of social and political environments on female students are incorporated as a basic tenet. Presents a specific course, *Introductory Social Science: The Social System*, that invites student self-involvement and provides an exercise in experiential learning. Discusses a second course, *Introductory Social Science: The Community*, that encourages students to move from the classroom mini-society to the local community. Emphasizes, generally, the need to transform the entire structure of courses and, specifically, the viability of teaching students to look to the self as a source of authority. Presents the key elements in Alverno's curricular change and offers syllabi for both courses.

162.    Thompson, Becky, and Tyagi Sangeeta. "Multicultural Education and the Sociological Imagination." *Teaching Sociology* 21 (April 1993): 192-196.

Applauds the influence of multiculturalism on the teaching of sociology that decries the countermovement that manifests itself in the conservative political-correctness movement. Explores this current backlash and its effects, especially on progressive sociologists who are instituting race, class, and gender consciousness into educational change. Analyzes the impact of (1) conservatives who criticize what they feel is a too-inclusive scholarship, (2) the challenge they pose to interdisciplinarity, and (3) the challenge they pose to the empowerment of current students interested in a more-inclusive curriculum. Also discusses some of the obstacles inside the academy that threaten developing multidimensional programs.

*Teacher Education*

163.    Atwater, Mary M., Kelly Radzik-Marsh, and Marilyn Strutchens, eds. *Multicultural Education: Inclusion of All.* Athens, GA: College of Education, The University of Georgia, 1994. 297 pp.

Aimed mainly at science and mathematics educators and teacher-education programs. Presents 14 essays arranged in 4 parts: (1) multiculturalism in teacher education programs (e.g., equity and the teaching of mathematics), (2) multiculturalism in learning and instruction (e.g., teaching and learning styles in science and math classrooms and interrelationships among gender, affect, and retention in science classrooms), (3) multiculturalism and assessment (e.g., the impact of standardized testing on children of color), and (4) family and societal influences on multiculturalism (e.g., mathematical empowerment and African-American families).

164.    Hicks, Reta D., and Eula E. Monroe. "The Infusion of Multicultural Education in Teacher Education Programmes

with Specific Focus on Reading Methods Courses." *Journal of Multilingual and Multicultural Development* 5 (2) (1984): 147-158.

Asserts the necessity of understanding multicultural as involving much more than racial diversity. Advances that a broader interpretation would include the poor and rich, handicapped and gifted, religious groups, as well as cultures of the world. Calls for the involvement of the total faculty in colleges of education to infuse multicultural concepts in programs of teacher preparation. Presents suggestions for implementation that involve three levels — college, departmental, and course. Directs emphasis toward integrating multicultural education into reading methods courses without harming basic content. Identifies practices that are already multicultural and suggests revision of selected topics in pre-service survey and practicum courses and in graduate foundations, diagnosis, and remediation courses.

165.    Hollins, Etta Ruth. "Debunking the Myth of a Monolithic White American Culture; or, Moving Toward Cultural Inclusion." *American Behavioral Scientist* 34 (2) (November/December 1990): 201-209.

Describes the process used in an educational foundations course to help preservice teachers, who likely are mainstream, view themselves as part of a culturally diverse society. Discusses the importance of designing teacher-preparation experiences that will bridge the gap between the experiences of teachers and students. Discusses a process of socialization in a course that emphasizes multiculturalism and uses as one of the main teaching strategies, the studying and sharing of personal family histories. Includes other pedagogical strategies, specific assignments and evaluation procedures. Assesses the course's impact especially on middle-class white students.

166.    Koch, Janice. "Elementary Science Education: Looking Through the Lens of Gender." *Initiatives* 55 (3) (1993): 67-71.

Examines the importance of solid scientific training for female elementary teachers, who outnumber males in this crucial area and must serve as science role models for female students. Emphasizes the necessity of elementary science methods courses providing and encouraging basic, hands-on exploratory experiences for females in science education. Describes some important elements for science-education students to be taught; allowing each student to discover his or her own abilities through science; providing connections between science and lived experiences, especially those of females; and providing informal and extracurricular learning experiences, to which research indicates that females tend to respond at an early age. Also discusses the need to emphasize female, as well as male, role models and issues about gender and science.

167.    Mason, Rachel. "Helping Student-Teachers Broaden Their Conceptions of Art Curricula." *Art Education* 39 (4) (July 1986): 46-51.

Examines the tendency of art-teacher training in Britain, and to a somewhat lesser degree, in America to be subject-specific, vocational, technical, and isolated from other school subjects or disciplines. Explores ways by which these programs can be broadened or extended to embrace more liberal or humane conceptions of the actual teaching of art in schools. Advocates a concerted effort to integrate art education with a range of other subjects and to explore the multicultural and multiethnic aspects of art that too often are slighted by traditional training and methodologies. Dissects the differences between essentialist and contextualist curriculum objectives and the attempts to integrate the two. Presents and explains how student-teachers can experiment with the four thematic modes of curriculum planning identified as characteristic of interdisciplinary practice. Reinforces the thesis that art specialists should use the context of art to enhance humanistic, environmental, or multicultural general education objectives.

168.    National Association for Bilingual Education. *Professional Standards for the Preparation of Bilingual/Multicultural Teachers.* Washington, DC: National Association for Bilingual Education, 1992.

Details the 1992 culmination of a 1989 formal resolution by the National Association for Bilingual Education calling for the development of national standards for bilingual/multicultural teacher preparation. Presents the six major standards and criteria for achievement associated with each standard: (1) institutional resources, coordination, and commitment; (2) recruitment, advisement, and retention of potential teachers; (3) bilingual/multicultural coursework and curriculum; (4) language proficiency in English and non-English languages and the abilities to teach in those languages; (5) field work and practicum experiences in bilingual/multicultural classrooms; and (6) life-long learning and commitment to professional involvement.

169.    Nicklin, Julie L. "Teacher-Education Programs Face Pressure to Provide Multicultural Training." *The Chronicle of Higher Education* 38 (11) (November 27, 1991): A1, A16.

Looks at the mounting pressures from a number of constituencies to provide greater multicultural training to future teachers who increasingly will be required to include issues of race and gender in their teaching. Gives examples of some specific recent developments: for example, a course at George Washington University for future literature teachers; a required course, *Multicultural Education for a Pluralistic Society,* for all students in teacher education at Sacramento State University; and though not required, a range of multicultural issues woven throughout the University of Maryland at College Park's teacher-education program, based on a recommendation by the Maryland State Department of Education several years earlier. Notes that many current programs are accelerations of efforts that began years ago and presents a variety of educators' responses to the heightened attention and initiatives. Examines some of the internal and external stimuli that have pressured for change and some of the problems that remain to be overcome.

170. Yepes-Baraya, Mario. "Developing Multicultural Curricula for Teacher Education: A Case Study from SUNY College at Fredonia." Paper presented at the conference on Multicultural Education: Programs and Strategies for Action, Springfield, IL, 1-3 April 1991. ERIC, ED 334303.

Describes *Multicultural Education: Teaching and Learning with Culturally Diverse Students*, a new course that is part of the teacher-education program at the State of New York College, Fredonia. Discusses the three key curriculum issues that guided design objectives: (1) maintain balance between the issues of American mainstream culture and those of minority groups, (2) introduce the principles of multicultural education and pedagogy used with minority group students, and (3) integrate theory and practice. Explains the integration of diverse components meant to balance course work with real-world conditions and the need for a complementary second semester to handle large amounts of material. Includes a bibliography, a description of the teacher-education program, a syllabus, two examinations, an advance organizer for unit one on the need to study multicultural education, and guidelines for a school unit.

## Interdisciplinary Fields

*American Studies*

171. Kessler-Harris, Alice. "Cultural Locations: Positioning American Studies in the Great Debate." *American Quarterly* 44 (3) (September 1992): 299-312.

Feels that American Studies as a discipline must first understand that what is often labeled as political correctness detracts from the issues surrounding multiculturalism. Asserts that the main issue is how cultural unity may be preserved while doing justice to the multiplicity of cultures within America. Asserts that to accomplish this balance we must redefine what is meant by identity. Attempts to reconcile the implications of new available knowledge with the current pressures generated by the traditional, continuing concept of American identity. Explores the historical development of American studies and discusses the necessity of seeing that constructing new national identities illustrates that democratic culture is a continuous, unending process. Discusses how American studies can view and utilize the multicultural enterprise as a potentially strengthening, as opposed to divisive, element in structuring curricula.

172.    Mazie, Margery, and others. "To Deconstruct Race, Deconstruct Whiteness." *American Quarterly* 45 (2) (June 1993): 281-94.

Examines a fall 1991 American Studies course entitled "Racialism and Inter-racialism in American Culture and Thought" taught at George Washington University. States that the main goal of the class was to refute the notion that in America, race presents continuous biological and historical components that rigidly and inevitably perpetuate division and animosity. Explores the pervasive belief that people with light skin tones and European ancestry hold an exclusive and superior racial identity. Explores, further, the assumption that the American concept of race is not really biologically meaningful. Examined in the course: (1) the nonbiological explanations for America's racialization, (2) the scientific arguments that buttress racializing actions, and (3) the ultimate falseness of notions of racial integrity. Presents ultimate falseness of notions of racial integrity. Presents the overall course pedagogy and process. Concludes that classrooms should not offer cultural histories that devolve into two simplistic racial dichotomies while at the same time offering a forum for the examination of the emotional involvement we all hold in our racial identities.

*Ethnic/Black Studies*

173.    Aldridge, Delores P. "Toward a New Role and Function of Black Studies in White and Historically Black Institutions." *The Journal of Negro Education* 53 (3) (Summer 1984): 359-367.

Proposes that black studies curricula be extended into a wider arena that concerns both the individual and the larger social environments in which blacks exist. Attempts to begin development of a general systems approach to curriculum expansion that encompasses black studies on both predominantly black or predominantly white campuses. Defines a general systems theory and uses it to defend the internationalizing of black studies, thus expanding the context within which these programs exist and grow.

174.    Alkalimat, Abdul, and others. *Introduction to Afro-American Studies: A Peoples College Primer*. Chicago, IL: Twenty-First Century Books and Publications, 1986. 391 pp.

Presented initially in 1973 as a course syllabus-study guide at Fisk University. After an introduction on the who, what, why, for whom of Afro-American studies, includes chapters on the Afro-American heritage (Africa before and after slave trade), colonialism and the slave trade, the slave experience, the emergence of the Afro-American nationality during the rural experience, the proletarianization of Afro-Americans during the urban experience, black workers and the labor movement, the black middle class, black culture and the arts, religion and the black church, black women and the family, education and the school in the black community, black power and the U.S. political system, civil rights and the struggle for democracy, nationalism and pan-Africanism, Marxism and black liberation, and present and future roles for blacks. Also includes a bibliography, a list of selected scholarly journals, and a list of bibliographical tools in Afro-American studies.

175.    Andersen, Margaret L. "Women's Studies/Black Studies: Learning from Our Common Pasts/Forging a Common

Future." In *Women's Place in the Academy: Transforming the Liberal Arts Curriculum,* edited by Marilyn R. Schuster and Susan R. Van Dyne, 62-72. Totowa, NJ: Rowman and Allanheld, 1985.

Explores the linkage between women's studies and black studies and asserts the overriding need for a strong alliance that unites the two in the challenge to transform the curriculum. Gives a brief look at the intertwined histories of both and provides a collaborative model for transformation.

176.    Anderson, Talmadge, ed. *Black Studies: Theory, Method and Cultural Perspectives.* Pullman: Washington State University Press, 1990. 227 pp.

Presents an interdisciplinary collection of contemporary essays. Includes eight sections: (1) introduction and overview, (2) research methodology and approaches (e.g., the emerging paradigm in black studies and appropriate and inappropriate research frameworks), (3) topics and issues in African and African-American history (e.g., historical consciousness and politics and pan-African consciousness), (4) sociological perspectives (e.g., the intellectual foundations of racism and a critical assessment of methodology), (5) psychology and the Afrocentric ethos (e.g., the Afrocentric theory of personality), (6) blacks and politics (e.g., electoral outcomes and policy impacts), (7) black economic perspectives (e.g., block affirmative action), and (8) African-American music and dance.

177.    Anderson, Talmadge. *Introduction to African American Studies: Cultural Concepts and Theory.* Dubuque, IA: Kendall/Hunt Publishing Company, 1993. 292 pp.

Gives a concise overview of black studies and African American heritage in America. Summarizes in chapter one the purpose(s), objectives, foundation, and philosophy of African-American studies. Discusses in chapter two the origin of black studies at San Francisco State College and explores contemporary concepts (e.g., Afrocentrism), new research paradigms, and analytical frameworks in the field. Presents the highlights of African-American history, sociological perspectives, black psychology, politics and African Americans, black economics, and African-American arts and humanities in the remaining chapters.

178. Baker, Houston A., Jr. *Black Studies, Rap, and the Academy*. Chicago, IL: The University of Chicago Press, 1993. 110 pp.

Presents a brief history of black studies, focusing particularly on its triumphs, setbacks, and major detractors. Looks at the influence of the political correctness debate on the discipline. Then, using rap music as a contemporary touchstone, plots the vitality and health of seminal scholars and black studies itself. Speculates on prospects for the discipline into the later 1990s.

179. Butler, Johnnella E. "Ethnic Studies: A Matrix Model for the Major." *Liberal Education* 77 (2) (March/April 1991): 26-32.

Proposes that all ethnic studies — black studies in particular — adopt a matrix-model approach to understanding and for curricular presentation. Is a connective, comparative, and interactive model that analyzes, for example, the black experience through an inclusive study of people of African ancestry in the United States, the Caribbean, and Latin America while, at the same time, considering race, class, ethnicity, and gender, all within the context of culture, politics, and social and economic expression. Includes an analysis of what she sees as the fragility of ethnic studies and a look at some specific programs and departments.

180. Butler, Johnnella E. *Black Studies: Pedagogy and Revolution*: A Study of Afro-American Studies and the Liberal Arts Tradition. Washington, DC: University Press of America, Inc., 1981. 154 pp.

Presents an overview of Afro-American studies and the liberal arts tradition through the discipline of Afro-American literature. Includes chapters on black studies and sensibility, using identity as the foundation for a pedagogy; the controversy of differing sensibilities; the cultural context of Afro-American reality; the ambivalent aesthetic of the Afro-American sensibility and Afro-American literature; and the pedagogy of revolution and black studies. Also includes a view of educational implications and a list of recommendations for further study, plus a bibliography and an extensive syllabus for a course on major black writers of fiction.

181.    Goodstein, Lynne, and LaVerne Gyant. "A Minor of Our Own: A Case for an Academic Program in Women of Color." *Women's Studies Quarterly* 18 (1 & 2) (Spring/Summer 1990): 39-45.

Discusses, specifically, the historical events and, generally, the cultural milieu that precipitated the development of an academic minor focusing on women of color at Pennsylvania State University, University Park. Analyzes the state of women of color in women's studies classrooms and the inadequate attention paid to the significant differences in history, culture, and experience among various subgroups of minority women. Gives specific structure, requirements, and course descriptions of the 18-credit minor and defends it as a link among women's, ethnic, and black studies.

182.    Hune, Shirley. "Opening the American Mind and Body: The Role of Asian American Studies." *Change* 21 (6) (November/December 1989): 56-63.

Traces the background and development of Asian American studies from its origin in the late 1960s to its increasingly successful and influential present status. Delineates both certain commonalities and important differences with other ethnic and women's studies and explores the ramifications of both. Discusses some of the academic and curricular impacts that Asian American studies has already had and speculates on new directions that may be taken. Includes a list of Asian/Pacific islander student groups and Asian American studies programs throughout the United States.

183.    James, Joy. "Reflections on Teaching: 'Gender, Race, & Class'." *Feminist Teacher* 5 (3) (Spring 1991): 9-15.

Examines the experience in the team-taught course *Gender, Race, and Class: Perspectives on Oppression, Power, and Liberation* at a midwestern public university. Looks at the composition of the team (four professors, three African-American women and one European-American man with degrees in social geography, psychology, political philosophy, and art/architecture) and some of the resulting implications. Gives a background on the epistemology and ethics underpinning the course and analyzes some of the problems encountered, including language/definitions and student resistance. Advances that resistance was caused by course content that was threatening, the uniqueness of the course, and the complexities of theory. Describes strategies and materials used and traces the movement of student response from resistance to ambivalence to transformation, and finally to general acceptance. Concludes with an analysis of the course, which received high ratings, as in offering an enlightened and democratic education.

184.    Lim, Shirley Geok-Lin. "Feminist and Ethnic Literary Theories in Asian American Literature." *Feminist Studies* 19 (3) (Fall 1993): 571-595.

Begins with a brief acknowledgment of the uneasiness between women's studies and ethnic studies, although these studies (including African-American and others) are often lumped together. Notes the transformation of women's studies being brought about by women of color whose issues extend beyond gender and power to race and ethnicity. Then describes the emergence of an Asian American canon in the 1970s and discusses in detail the texts and anthologies important in this development. Concludes with a brief look at texts that address Asian American feminism and the intersection of ethnic and feminist identities.

185.    Lim, Shirley Geok-Lin. "Asian-American Literature: Race, Class, Gender, and Sexuality." *Multicultural Review* 3 (2) (June 1994): 46-51.

Discusses the various challenges in selecting works for an *Introduction to an Asian-American Literature Course*. Objectives include breaking the popular stereotypes of Asian Americans and introducing the heterogeneity of national-origin communities. Presents the curricular movement from the emphasis on race and equal representation among authors to course selections that present analyses of gender and class issues. Discusses the need for, and difficulties in, including sexual identity as a curricular component in Asian-American literature. References several leading works in each category.

186.    Roper, Larry D., and William E. Sedlacek. "Student Affairs Professionals in Academic Roles: A Course on Racism." *NASPA Journal* 26 (1) (1988): 27-32.

Proposes that to contribute to the mission of student intellectual development and transmission of knowledge, student affairs professionals must define their functions in terms that are academic and must contribute to the educational processes of their institutions. Describes the development in 1985 of "Education and Racism," a course designated as part of the required Advanced Studies and taught by student affairs staff. Discusses the multicultural nature of the course and presents its goals, contents, and teaching methods (including segments on conveying and analyzing information, understanding racial attitudes, and changing behaviors), and outcomes. Assesses the overall course impact.

187.    Tierney, William G., and Clara Sue Kidwell, eds. "Special Report: American Indians in Higher Education," *Change* 23 (2) (March/April 1991): 4-46.

Includes articles on the history of conflict, the reappearance of the Native American in the college curriculum, a workable college intervention program, a portrait of state-of-the-art Indian education in Minnesota, strategies for empowering native voices in higher education, and the early Indian School Movement.

188.    Townsend, Barbara K. "Feminist Scholarship and the Study of Women in Higher Education." *Initiatives* 55 (1) (December 1992): 1-9.

Enumerates the continuing ways in which feminist scholarship has altered and redefined the academy. Reviews some of the major contemporary theories and gives an overview of what is meant by feminist content and methodology, plus some future implications for the study of women in higher education. Notes the varying definitions of feminism and discusses four of the major theoretical orientations that underpin feminist thought: liberal, cultural, radical, and socialist (also looks briefly at psychoanalytical, postmodernist, and poststructuralist). Assesses the content and methodology (i.e., epistemological basis and qualitative orientation) of feminist scholarship and points out the need for a reexamination of current androcentric research paradigms.

## International/Global Education

189.    Groennings, Sven, and David S. Wiley, eds. *Group Portrait: Internationalizing the Disciplines*. New York: The American Forum, 1990. 468 pp.

Presents and defends the need for the developers of university and college curricula to be acutely aware of the growing significance of intercultural contexts. Looks at seven disciplines in particular: (1) geography (e.g., culture and nationality), (2) history (e.g., the comparative world history approach and common goals for world history courses), (3) political science (e.g., American and non-American, the integration of American and comparative politics, the international component of political science curricula, and political science concepts in an introductory course on international relations), (4) sociology (e.g., social systems as world systems), (5) psychology (e.g., cross-cultural psychology, psychology and its world context), (6) journalism and mass communication (e.g., revamping the journalism curriculum, integrating international perspectives into research methods course, and learning from African models), and (7) philosophy (e.g., philosophy and world citizenship, philosophy and international problems, overcoming ethnocentrism in the philosophy classroom. Includes a bibliography on international perspectives for the undergraduate curriculum.

190.    Raby, Rosalind Latiner, ed. *International Master Modules for Internationalizing the Curriculum: A General Catalogue*. Los Angeles: Los Angeles Community College District, Institute for International Programs, 1991. ERIC, ED 336150.

         Presents short summaries of more than 175 International Master Modules encompassing over 60 disciplines and subject areas. Also includes courses that reflect an international perspective. Discusses the rationale for developing classes in international studies and introducing international components into existing classes. Groups the modules into 46 alphabetized disciplinary categories.

191.    Stitzel, Judith, Ed Pytlik, and Kate Curtis. "'Only Connect': Developing a Course on Women in International Development." *Women's Studies Quarterly* 13 (2) (Summer 1985): 33-35.

         Examines the background, planning, and content of a course, Women in International Development, considered one of the most significant accomplishments of the Women's Studies Program at West Virginia University in academic year 1981-82. Discusses the cooperation between women's studies and technology education in producing a course that includes women in development and acknowledges women's agricultural labor and explores their *physical* and *social* as well as economic well-being and equity. Presents the overarching course objectives and a discussion of the general movement through the class, including projects, case studies, guest-speaker presentations, and coordinated evening lectures. Examines the positive results of a course that attracted international, as well as American students, and presents a list of required texts, reserve readings, other course-content readings, and the syllabus.

## Women's studies

192. Butler, Johnnella E., and John C. Walter, eds. *Transforming the Curriculum: Ethnic Studies and Women's Studies*. Albany, NY: State University of New York Press, 1991. 341 pp.

Divides the essays into four parts: (1) the interrelationships between ethnic studies and women's studies. (Explores the difficult dialogue of curriculum transformation, funding women's studies, private-foundation grants to ethnic studies between 1972-1988, and a model institute for integrating women of color into undergraduate American literature and history courses.) (2) ethnic studies and women's studies in the liberal arts. (Looks at essentials in pedagogy and theory [e.g., teaching white women, racism, and antiracism in a women's studies program; the transformation of a survey course in Afro-American history; African-American studies and Chicano studies; and Jewish studies]), (3) ethnic studies and women's studies in the liberal arts: scholarship implications (e.g., gender in the context of race and class, Asian-American literary traditions, understanding radical elements in American Indian fiction, and the status of Armenian-American women), and (4) a black feminist perspective on the academy. Includes a critical assessment of Allan Bloom's *The Closing of the American Mind*.

193. Chamberlain, Mariam K., and Alison Bernstein. "Philanthropy and the Emergence of Women's Studies." *Teachers College Record* 93 (3) (Spring 1992): 556-568.

Details the seminal importance of philanthropic contributions to the growth and institutionalization of women's study. Looks at such key donors and supporters as, for example, the Ford Foundation, the Rockefeller Foundation, the Carnegie Corporation, the Charles Stewart Mott Foundation, the Andrew W. Mellon Foundation, and the Lilly Endowment, and assesses their importance in assisting in the growth not only of women's studies but also of national associations and the essential corollary element of journals and textbooks. Examines the part these organizations have played in pushing forward curriculum integration, the mainstreaming of minority women's studies, and a recognition of the global significance of women's studies as a scholarly activity. Summarizes the overall positive philanthropic impact on the discipline, particularly over the last two decades.

194.     Chamberlain, Mariam K. "Multicultural Women's Studies in the United States." *Women's Studies Quarterly* 22 (3 & 4) (Fall/Winter 1994): 215-225.

Provides a succinct overview of the development and current status of women's studies. Discusses the origins of women's studies in higher education in the 1970s and the factors contributing to its institutionalization. Discusses the importance of external funding and women's research centers. Briefly reviews the early desire for, but difficulties with, developing a multiethnic perspective in women's studies. Describes the role of the National Council for Research on Women and the movement to mainstream women's studies and minority women's studies.

195.     Culley, Margaret, and Catherine Portuges, eds. *Gendered Subjects: The Dynamics of Feminist Teaching*. Boston: Routledge & Kegan Paul, 1985. 284 pp.

Divides the essays into seven parts: (1) frameworks and definitions (e.g., classroom pedagogy and the new scholarship on women, women's studies and taking women students seriously), (2) transforming the disciplines (e.g., feminist pedagogy as a subversive activity, a feminist perspective on the study of law, and a theoretical model for the feminist classroom), (3) teaching across race and gender (e.g., a black feminist in a white, predominately male English department and a male feminist in a women's college classroom), (4) experience as text (e.g., life in the feminist classroom and teaching black women), (5) theory as text (e.g., teaching feminist theory, gender in cinema), (6) the possible contradiction of authority in the feminist classroom and anger in the introductory women's studies classroom), and (7) communication across differences (e.g., everywoman's studies, combating the marginalization of black women in the classroom, and teaching the feminist minority). Also includes a selected bibliography.

196.    Davidman, Lynn, and Shelly Tenebaum, eds. *Feminist Perspectives on Jewish Studies.* New Haven, CT: Yale University Press, 1994. 281 pp.

Provides a comprehensive look at the integration of feminist scholarship into various disciplines encompassed by Jewish studies. Includes chapters on Jewish studies and theology, philosophy, modern Jewish history, sociology, anthropology, American-Jewish literature, modern Hebrew literature, rabbinics, and film. Begins with a concise overview of the conceptual and methodological concerns of feminism and their relationship to Jewish feminist thought and studies. Reports feminist impact as the greatest in anthropology but, also, as recently emerging in American Jewish literature and Jewish history. Notes that, overall, the chapter authors report limited incorporation of feminist works and perspectives.

197.    de Groot, Joanna, and Mary Maynard, eds. *Women's Studies in the 1990s: Doing Things Differently?* New York: St. Martin's Press, 1993. 182 pp.

Includes eight essays on selected topics: (1) context in the next decade, (2) the use of researcher personal response in feminist methodology, (3) a concept for exploring women's political perceptions, (4) the cross purposes of literature and women's studies, (5) problems of theory and method in feminist history, (6) the significance of cultural relativism, (7) approaches to feminist theory and politics, and (8) problems and possibilities for women's studies in the 1990s.

198.     Farnham, Christie, ed. *The Impact of Feminist Research in the Academy*. Bloomington, IN: Indiana University Press, 1987. 228 pp.

Divides its essays into four parts: (1) gender as an analytical category (the struggle to reshape our thinking about gender in anthropology and women's history and the rewriting of history), (2) methodological moves from the margin to the center (toward a paradigm shift in the academy and in religious studies, remapping development and the power of divergent data, and feminist research and psychology), (3) the persistence of stereotypes (a polemic on sex-differences research, feminist economics, the relationship between the political socialization of women and the political socialization of people, and revising the literary canon through reflections on black women writers), and (4) implications for the paradigm (the impact of women's studies on sociology and literature).

199.     Frankenberg, Ruth. "Teaching 'White Women, Racism and Anti-Racism' in a Women's Studies Program." In *Transforming the Curriculum: Ethnic Studies and Women's Studies*, edited by Johnnella E. Butler and John C. Walter, 89-109. Albany, NY: State University of New York Press, 1991.

Explains the institutional environment that made possible a course examining white women as racially positioned actors. Discusses the rationale for the course and the questions it sought to answer. Speculates on the course's impact generally on the Women's Studies Program and the need for women's studies, overall, to become more inclusive, less focused on the white and the middle class. Presents the specific structure of the courses; the interaction of teacher, teaching assistants, and students; the syllabus; and a course bibliography.

200. Fritsche, JoAnn M., and others. *Toward Excellence & Equity: The Scholarship on Women as a Catalyst for Change in the University.* Orono, Maine: University of Maine at Orono, 1984. 335 pp.

Includes chapters on developing support for a curriculum inclusion project (e.g., why, how to start, major steps, convincing others, identifying co-leaders, influencing opinion leaders and key administrators, naming the project, planning a pilot project, and requesting and securing funds), implementing the pilot project, ensuring project continuation (securing internal and external funding, involving both feminist and nonfeminist faculty and staff, establishing criteria, and promoting change in institutional policies and practices), and risks and rewards of curriculum integration, responses and critiques from students and colleagues (five faculty members' experiences), and policies and politics. Also included are a sample evaluation instrument, a faculty log of self-evaluation, a sample student questionnaire, an assessment of student response, and a bibliography.

201. Hatton, Ed. "The Future of Women's Studies: A Ford Foundation Workshop Report." *Women's Studies Quarterly* 22 (3 & 4) (Fall/Winter 1994): 256-264.

Describes a 1992 Ford Foundation workshop attended by over thirty academics to discuss the future of women's studies. Provides informative overviews from the presenters on four panels: (1) the current status of women's studies; (2) current research and teaching about women in the United States; (3) connections with international women's studies; and (4) academic scholarship, public policy, and activism. Includes information from leaders in the fields, such as Beverly Guy-Sheftall, Paula Rothenberg, Alice Kessler-Harris, Florence Howe, and Johnnella Butler, to name a few.

202.    Hinds, Hilary, Ann Phoenix, and Jackie Stacey, eds. *Working Out: New Directions for Women's Studies*. Washington, DC: The Falmer Press, 1992. 208 pp.

Includes 16 papers from the 1991 Women's Studies Network (UK) annual conference. Deals with the politics and practice of women's studies, the issue of commonalities and differences between women, and theoretical developments that challenge future directions. In a separate chapter, Chris Corrin examines the education of girls and women, the support for women's studies within academic circles, and the emergence of feminist theory and women's studies in East-Central Europe. Papers address a variety of complex issues in feminist theory and practice and their relationship to women's studies as a relatively new discipline.

203.    Howe, Florence, and Mariam K. Chamberlain, eds. "Women's Studies: A World View." *Women's Studies Quarterly* 22 (3 & 4) (Fall/Winter 1994): 1-269.

Grew out of the Fifth International Interdisciplinary Congress on Women held in Costa Rica in 1993. Includes papers from leading women scholars in 13 countries, and each, generally, addresses the relationship among women's studies and the women's movement and the status of women in their respective countries. Organizes this special volume by decades and programs beginning in each: 1970s-Canada, United States, India, New Zealand, Japan, and Argentina; 1980s-West Indies, Israel, Taiwan, and Costa Rica; and 1990s-Russia, Poland, Kenya, and Lithuania. Notes that programs begun in the 1980s are still more marginalized than older programs and less able to turn to concerns at the primary and secondary level. Expresses concern over the distance in more-established programs between theorizing and the needs and concerns of the women's movement. Also includes papers from the 1993 European conference sponsored by the Network on Interdisciplinary Women's Studies in Europe to compare the development of multicultural women's studies in the United States with efforts in Europe. Concludes with a report from a Ford Foundation workshop on the future of women's studies in the United States and worldwide.

204.    Ibrahim, Farah A. "A Course on Asian-American Women: Identity Development Issues." *Women's Studies Quarterly* 20 (1 & 2) (Spring/Summer 1992): 41-58.

Reviews how a course focusing on Asian-American women can be structured using sociohistorical and cultural information and a psychological intervention to facilitate the gender/racial/cultural identity development of Asian-American women and women in general. Examines the literature on gender identity development models for women and the issues that address the psychology of women. Presents racial/cultural identity development models that lead to an integrated model for Asian-American women's gender and cultural identity development. Includes extensive references, course description, course process, required texts, supplemental readings, course requirements, and course schedule.

205.    Johnson, Rhoda E. Barge, ed. *Women's Studies in the South.* Dubuque, IA: Kendall/Hunt Publishing Company, 1991. 315 pp.

Describes the text as based on over fifteen years of feminist process for students and faculty at the University of Alabama, Tuscaloosa. States that the southern location and culture has led women's studies to look at feminism in the South. Divides into four units: (1) the development of women's studies and the feminist movement (e.g., definition of *feminist pedagogy*, the personal as political, the possibility of feminist men, women's studies in the Southeast, the separate paths to liberation of black and white women, and an argument against feminism), (2) the ways in which we construct *woman* (e.g., introduction from de Beauvoir's *The Second Sex*, southern women's autobiography, conceptual and normative considerations of stereotypes, comments on being a black woman Episcopal priest, and dilemmas of the Jewish feminist), (3) institutionalized oppression (e.g., ethical issues of feminist scholarship; the importance of class awareness in social work practice; women, ordination, and the Christian church; arguments about abortion; and understanding battered women), and (4) an examination of scholarship and activism (e.g., cultural crossroads, moving from theory to practice, analyzing the barriers to black-white women's coalitions, and issues and approaches to organizing women).    Also includes a list of suggested additional readings.

206.    Koster-Lossack, Angelika, and Tobe Levin, eds. "Women's Studies in Europe." *Women's Studies Quarterly* 20 (3 & 4) (Fall\Winter 1992): 15-163.

Presents a comparative look at women's studies counterparts in Europe. Includes the countries of Belgium, Bulgaria, France, Germany, Ireland, Italy, The Netherlands, the Nordic countries, Spain, and the United Kingdom. Explores such topics as specific programs; international cooperative efforts; relationships among women's studies; women's political movement and the state; feminist research; thematic portraits; and feminist historiography. Discusses GRACE: the European Community Women's Studies Database; and Networking: the European Network for Women's Studies (ENWS) and Women's International Studies Europe (WISE).

207.    National Women's Studies Association Task Force for the Association of American Colleges. *Liberal Learning and the Women's Studies Major.* Washington, DC: Association of American Colleges, 1991. unpaged

Examines both the philosophical and practical contexts of women's studies. Looks at the general course composition and some of the problems that have characterized the women's studies major. Also offers models for the major and introductory courses, as well as analyses of courses in feminist theory, race and gender, and women and science. Offers a set of recommendations for making positive changes in existing programs or for initiating new programs. Has an

extensive appendix that includes models for the major;
courses in introductory women's studies, feminist theory,
race and gender, and women and science; a senior seminar
or capstone course; guidelines for cross-listing courses; and
a bibliography on feminist pedagogy.

208.    Paludi, Michele, and Gertrude A. Steuernagel, eds.
        *Foundations for a Feminist Restructuring of the Academic
        Disciplines*. New York: The Haworth Press, 1990. 276 pp.

Gives the experiences of women who are involved in
curriculum transformation and feminist pedagogy. Presents
a variety of educational environments established in the
academy. Includes articles on feminism and women's
studies, the images and the reality of women's lives, a
literature perspective on the images of women, views from
the discipline of history, an economic perspective, the image
of women in political science, images of women in
psychology, and reflections from the health care system. Also
includes an index and an extensive directory of curriculum-
integration resources.

209.    Rao, Aruna, ed. *Women's Studies International: Nairobi and
        Beyond*. New York: The Feminist Press at the City University
        of New York, 1991. 349 pp.

Includes essays arranged in five categories: (1) theory
and learning (gender as a means of historical analysis, an
alternative perspective on education and rural women, and
new models for research and policy on women and income
in the Third World), (2) teaching and strategies for change (in
Latin America and India), (3) policy (linking research with
policy and action and integrating gender in research and
policy for development in Thailand), (4) institutionalization
(growth and institutionalization in the United States and the
incorporation of gender issues in development training), and
(5) new models and priorities for research on women (in
Latin American, Southeast Asia, and the Caribbean). Also
includes an extensive chapter on program descriptions (in
Argentina, Canada, England, India, Lebanon, Mexico and

Netherlands, and between Thailand and Canada and at The Ohio State University. Gives a resource list on both research and teaching about women.

210.    Richardson, Diane, and Victoria Robinson, eds. *Thinking Feminist: Key Concepts in Women's Studies.* New York: Guilford Press, 1993. 421 pp.

Addresses in 14 chapters many issues important in feminist scholarship: for example, racism, sexuality and male dominance, violence toward women, representation in popular culture, women and family, motherhood and reproduction, education, women at work, and women and protest. Begins with an informative chapter introducing women's studies and its students, perspectives, and pedagogy and then addresses debates within the field. Concludes in the introduction with a call for reconnecting theory and action to empower girls and older women worldwide, to support diversity and commonalities internationally, and to reach the goal of a global feminism.

211.    Staudt, Kathleen. "Women in Development: Courses and Curriculum Integration." *Women's Studies Quarterly* 14 (3 & 4) (Fall/Winter 1986): 21-28.

Describes an interdisciplinary field, Women in Development, based in social science and drawn primarily from anthropology, sociology, and development and women's studies and secondarily from economics, political science/public administration, and geography. Presents a range of materials, theories, core directions and themes, texts and supplements, activities, and projects for potential courses in this field. Describes the reliance on a woman-centered approach, tempered by a respect for differences among women or between women and men. Discusses the need for experiential diversity and the clear recognition of the central force of politics and bureaucracy both in understanding women's roles and status and in structuring formal courses. Includes suggested readings, both in general and in relation to specific counties and areas outside the United States.

212.    Stimpson, Catherine R., and Nina Kressner Cobb. *Women's Studies in the United States*. New York: Ford Foundation, 1986. 77 pp.

Presents an outside review and assessment of nationwide efforts in women's studies and places the field in a broader context. Views women's studies not only as part of the tradition of curricular reform, but also as a response to complex historical circumstances: the political dissent of the 1960s, demographic and educational changes, and the rise of the women's movement. Includes chapters on the development of women's studies, institutionalization of the field of study, issues and approaches, achievements and challenges, and the future of women's studies. Also includes a thematic selected bibliography.

213.    Treichler, Paula A., Cheris Kramarae, and Beth Stafford, eds. *For Alma Mater: Theory and Practice in Feminist Scholarship*. Urbana, IL: University of Illinois Press, 1985. 450 pp.

Among other essays, includes difference and continuity in feminist criticism, feminism and critical theory, the maturing of Chicana poetry in the 1980s, feminism in linguistics, interdisciplinary studies and a feminist community, refusing the legacy of institutional racism and sexism, recent directions in women's history, failures of androcentric studies of women's education in the third world, the arcane nature of men and their institutions, resources for the Chicana feminist scholar, and the implications of being a feminist academic. Also includes an assessment of current library research in women's studies.

214.    Williamson, Susan G., Nicole Hahn Rafter, and Amy Cohen-Rose. "Everyone Wins: A Collaborative Model for Mainstreaming Women's Studies." *The Journal of Academic Librarianship* 15 (1) (1989): 20-23.

Presents the collaborative model, an approach that gives professors the opportunity to request the aid of student researchers who are paid to produce bibliographies of women's studies materials for individual courses under the guidance of library personnel. Describes the initiation of the model at Swarthmore College and its later development at Northeastern University, both prompted, to some extent, by student frustration at the inability to find sufficient materials for research beyond the class syllabi. Details the process for selecting student researchers and faculty, student-assistant instruction, methods of integrating the material into courses, dissemination of research results, project evaluation, and some attendant problems. Concludes with some of the curricular effect of such a collaboration and its potential for use in other areas, such as black studies.

# EVALUATION AND ASSESSMENT

Planning, implementation, and evaluation compose three major dimensions of curricular development. Over the past three decades, the main thrust in multicultural education has been on planning and implementing curricular change. Activities included assessing the current status of underrepresented groups in the curriculum, identifying areas for change, organizing workshops and materials, and developing strategies to integrate "new knowledge" into existing courses while simultaneously constructing new fields of study.

The intensity of these dual thrusts of planning and implementation is reflected in the preponderance of literature in these veins. Numerous articles advance the philosophical, cultural, and demographic rationales for curricular transformation in the academy. Similarly, the sustained focus on implementation is reflected in the numerous case studies describing curricular change across institutions and in specific disciplines. As the literature reveals, at the forefront of curriculum transformation projects across the nation are leaders in women's studies.

African-American studies, however, opened the way in the 1960s for the new scholarship and was followed shortly thereafter by courses and programs organized around the emerging feminist perspectives. After two decades of sustained growth, the emerging fields only now are maturing to the point of asking questions of impact and effectiveness, both internally and in the established disciplines. Thus, the literature of assessment and evaluation in multicultural education is limited in both quantity and scope.

The evaluation studies, at least those reported in the literature, address one of three fundamental questions: what is the impact of multiculturalism on curricula in general? what is the impact of multiculturalism in specific disciplines? and what is the impact on student learning? Unsurprisingly, reliable answers to these complex and broad questions are not yet available, and unifying perspectives regarding the impact of multiculturalism either on curriculum or on students have not developed.

The 1991 survey of colleges and universities by Levine and Cureton was called the "first-of-its kind" and suggests that the claims of neither the multiculturalists nor the traditionalists are true; rather, the authors conclude that curricular change is widespread but has been affected by add-ons rather than substitutions in the established canon. In a similar assessment study, the Association of American Colleges surveyed member institutions for the presence of international education in the curriculum and found a wide variety of activities classified as global or international programming. Although both studies documented the *presence* of new curricular thrusts, neither attempted to measure impact or effectiveness.

The impact of multiculturalism at the disciplinary level poses a similar problem. The traditionalists claim that the long-established disciplines decline in integrity and quality when minority and feminist perspectives, and their accompanying materials that have not stood "the test of time," are forced into the curriculum. The reformers, however, describe an androcentric, Eurocentric curriculum, strongly resistant to multiple perspectives with only limited change in content and pedagogy. Again, at the disciplinary level the competing claims cannot be resolved; however, recent studies begin the search for more systematic evidence of impact and change.

For example, in the early 1990s curricular change in upper-level English literature courses was examined in a survey by the Modern Language Association, and history and biology were each examined in books issued as part of Twayne Publishers newly established series "Impact of Feminism on the Arts and Sciences." These studies suggest that although changes have occurred, the shifts are largely at the periphery of the disciplines and, as such, are limited in depth and significant impact.

At the close of the twentieth century, and as the emerging disciplines become better established, women's studies and African-American studies are beginning to ask serious questions about themselves, their "canons," impact on students, and the effectiveness of these programs nationwide. For example, in the late 1980s the Ford Foundation commissioned several consultants to examine the field of black studies in the United States to assess their current status, present strengths, and future needs. The result, *Three Essays: Black Studies in the United States*, was published in 1990. At about the same time, the National Women's Studies Association, with a grant from the Fund for the Improvement of

Postsecondary Education, launched a three-year research project that culminated in publication of *The Courage to Question: Women's Studies and Student Learning* and yielded a second volume, *Students at the Center: Feminist Assessment*, which specifically addresses issues of assessment. Luebke and Reilly (1995) continue the interest in student outcomes with publication of *Women's Studies Graduates: The First Generation* that reports findings from the first national survey of graduates of women's studies.

The limited number of publications focusing on evaluation in the multicultural domain should not be interpreted as a complete absence of program evaluation. Programs in global education, women's studies, and ethnic studies are not professional programs; consequently, they are not subject to specialized accrediting that prescribes specific evaluation activities at regularly established intervals, as in fields such as nursing and business. Rather, programs and courses in the emerging areas of interest, like most programs in the arts and sciences, are subject to internally established procedures for course evaluation, program review, and student evaluation. These evaluations, however, are rarely reported in the literature.

Additionally, the descriptive literature suggests that curricular changes in multicultural education have been, and are being, made through formative evaluation of course content, teaching methods, and student assessment. Additionally, these results are shared with colleagues on other campuses through informal and formal means, such as networks, workshops, and conferences.

The studies cited above are significant first steps in the evaluation and assessment cycle of program development. From these studies will come more refined assessments and an even closer examination of who is doing what, why, and how well. The evaluation reports that are emerging in the 1990s reflect a maturing of the fields and an attempt to step beyond course creation and program expansions to the wider concerns of program impact, student learning, and national progress.

## Surveys and Studies: Quantitative and Qualitative

215.    Brossard, Carlos A. "Classifying Black Studies Programs."
        *The Journal of Negro Education* 53 (3) (Summer 1984): 278-295.

        Analyzes some of the most significant problems that
        caused the failure of early black studies programs to secure
        academic credence and institutional validity. Examines the
        growing body of how performance is demonstrated,
        criticizes inexact measurement and conceptual confusions,
        and proposes clear research and demonstration techniques
        to allow a more fair evaluation of individual programs.
        Offers an analysis of (1) specific structural issues in the
        development of black studies and (2) both quantitative and
        qualitative evaluation measures. Presents for evaluating
        black studies programs a new mixed model that consists of
        three interrelated tiers: (1) structural issues in program
        development at particular institutional settings, (2) some
        external validation approaches, and (3) some organizational
        process data that describe actual organizational behaviors.

216.    Carnegie Foundation for the Advancement of Teaching.
        "Change Trendlines." *Change* 24 (1) (January/February 1992):
        49-52.

        Provides information on multicultural additions to
        higher education curricula. Reports the number of higher
        education faculty teaching in selected course areas (1990); the
        percentage of institutions reporting that general education
        requirements call for a least one course in four areas of
        multicultural education (1970 and 1985); and, the percentage
        of four-year colleges and universities requiring a course in
        each area (1990). Reports the number of four-year colleges
        and universities offering bachelor's degrees in selected fields
        (1975 to 1990), and the number of degrees conferred by
        colleges and universities in selected fields (1983 and 1988).
        Discusses the implications of the data for more extensive
        curricular change.

217. Carrillo, Teresa. "Promoting Multicultural Dissertation Research in a Eurocentric University." *American Behavioral Scientist* 34 (2) (November/December 1990): 181-187.

Details the difficulties encountered by a doctoral student in political science at a large, private institution. Included are such impediments as a too-rigid adherence to quantitative methodologies, even though numerous topics lend themselves to qualitative research; a too-strict reliance on written documents and published statistics for data, even with a subject population who rely on the oral tradition or are illiterate, lacking in formal education, and work outside formal vocational structures; a lack of qualified mentors for multicultural projects; and the marginal status of multicultural studies generally. Offers suggestions for promoting multicultural dissertation research.

218. Colon, Alan K. "Critical Issues in Black Studies: A Selective Analysis." *The Journal of Negro Education* 53 (3) (1984): 268-277.

Discusses the evolution of black studies in terms of scholarly intentions, critical direction, and historical perspective/continuity. Proposes a greater internal emphasis on outstanding black scholars and on their scholarly productions and a movement away from politics. Calls for a multifaceted development of black studies, including traditional white institutions, historically black institutions, and in important, alternative community-based institutions. Presents the results and implications of a survey of the directors of black studies programs at ten institutions.

219. Franklin, Phyllis, Bettina J. Huber, and David Laurence. "Continuity and Change in the Study of Literature." *Change* 24 (1) (January/February 1992): 42-48.

Analyzes the anecdotal evidence that implies that content and teaching methodologies have changed rather dramatically in upper-level English literature — one of the disciplines most amenable to the effects of multicultural curricular change. Uses the Modern Language Association's 1990 biennial survey of a stratified random sample of English departments (571 responses) to assess the true state of upper-level English literature courses. Includes tabular information, accompanied by analyses of those who, for example, have added newer, selected works; have added less commonly taught authors; who have incorporated new theoretical approaches; and who acknowledge that selected theoretical approaches affect their teaching. Utilizes results and their implications to criticize the validity of the "widely circulated assertions of dramatic change in the teaching of literature."

220.    Harris, Robert L. Jr., Darlene Clark Hine, and Nellie McKay. *Three Essays: Black Studies in the United States.* New York: The Ford Foundation, 1990. 29 pp.

        Presents essays by scholars who were invited to survey selected black studies departments, programs, institutes, and centers judged to be generally representative of Afro-American and Africana studies in the United States and to evaluate their capacities and strengths and assess their future needs. Includes essays concerning the intellectual and institutional development of Africana studies, an overview of black studies programs, and an analysis of black studies in the Midwest.

221.    Kelleher, Ann, and Jane Margaret O'Brien. "Surveying AAC Members: Planning for Global and International Education." *Liberal Education* 77 (5) (November/December 1991): 30-43.

        Presents the results of an Association of American Colleges (AAC) survey intended to evaluate the curricular content of member institutions for inclusion of global and international instruction. Also identifies the programs and activities through which global and international education is encouraged and achieved. Analyzes responses from 367 institutions in four broad areas: (1) geographical areas and issue content included in the curriculum, (2) approaches to curricular and faculty development, (3) suggestions of ways that AAC might support institutional efforts, and (4) identification of innovative and distinctive programs. Reveals that the areas of Central and Eastern Europe/USSR, Western Europe, Anglo-America (U.S., Canada), and Latin America led in number of courses. Also shows that respondents were generally unfamiliar with other institutions' programs. Part four includes detailed overviews of six specific programs: California State University, Long Beach; Goshen College; Kalamazoo College; Michigan State University; Warren Wilson College; Whitworth College.

222. Ladson-Billings, Gloria. "Beyond Multicultural Illiteracy." *The Journal of Negro Education* 60 (2) (1991): 147-157.

Presents an overview of the hotly contested debate over the efficacy of multicultural additions/changes to the traditional Eurocentric approach to curriculum and pedagogy. Uses a pretest and posttest in an undergraduate teacher-education course, Introduction to Teaching in a Multicultural Society, to assess and analyze the students' awareness — or ignorance — of significant terms and concepts connected with multicultural ideas, issues, events, and personalities. Gives details of class structure, activities, and awareness prior to and following student assessment. Offers suggestions for moving beyond multicultural illiteracy.

223. Lampe, Philip. "The Problematic Nature of an Ethnic Studies Program: A Sociological Perspective." *The Social Studies* 70 (4) (July/August 1979): 179-185.

Serves as an early background analysis of the potential and some problems associated with the then-new ethnic studies. Explores both theoretical and practical problems and offers prescriptive opinions about, for example, faculty selection, preferential pay, and hiring criteria. Includes results of original and follow-up questionnaires — one set sent to 60 academic deans and one sent to students at two Texas institutions — that probed a number of fundamental areas, including need for such programs, primary program function or orientation, faculty selection criteria, and ultimate goals.

224.    Levine, Arthur, and Jeannette Cureton. "The Quiet Revolution: Eleven Facts About Multiculturalism and the Curriculum." *Change* 24 (1) (January/February 1992): 25-29.

Reports the findings of a 1991 survey of 270 colleges and universities stratified by Carnegie type. Examines the extent to which respondents (196) engaged in specific multicultural activities and curriculum practices. Attempts, thus, to go beyond competing claims about the efficacy of multiculturalism and develop a picture of the real impact of this phenomenon on higher education curricula. Includes 6 tables of survey data and discussions of the 11 most salient facts that emerge from this analysis. Shows, for example, that new material added to existing courses is the most often reported curricular change, and that approximately one-half of the respondents have a multicultural general education requirement. Explains the survey methodology and offers some, at least, tentative conclusions about higher education's accommodation of multiculturalism in the curriculum.

225.    Luebke, Barbara F., and Mary Ellen Reilly. *Women's Studies Graduates: The First Generation*. New York: Teachers College Press, 1995. 207 pp.

Reports that a comprehensive national study of women's studies graduates has not been published and presents the responses from 89 study participants (25%), representing 43 women's studies programs, to a sample survey of graduates nationwide. Asks the questions, what do you do with a women's studies major? what are the backgrounds of the graduates? what are they doing now? and what impact did women's studies have on their personal and professional lives? Gives complete demographic descriptions of respondents and presents by name their individual stories in their *own voices*. Notes that much more needs to be done in the area of diversity (i.e., identifying where race and ethnicity will be addressed in the curriculum). Includes a chapter of advice to students, faculty, and administrators. Cites the widely used introductory course in women's studies as the single most important source for majors. Mentions, also, the importance of courses in the traditional disciplines with *gender*, *woman*, or *feminist* in the title. Summarizes important student outcomes as being empowered; gaining self-confidence; developing critical thinking skills; discovering the intersections of race, class, and gender; and experiencing community. Concludes that women's studies is a rigorous academic discipline that enables graduates to succeed in various professions and to go on to graduate-level work.

226. McCabe, Lester Thomas. "The Development of a Global Perspective During Participation in Semester at Sea: A Comparative Global Education Program." *Educational Review* 46 (3) (1994): 275-286.

Presents the results of a study examining the impact of a semester-at-sea program on students' development of a global perspective. Provides details of the research site, the methods and data analysis, and results. Sponsored by the Institute for Shipboard Education and the University of Pittsburgh, uses participant (n=23) observation, interviews, and student journals in the presemester and postsemester assessments. Describes five analytical dimensions used in interpreting a global perspective. Discusses the influence of preprogram beliefs and values on change during the learning experiences. Finds that sound curricular offerings and quality faculty members are essential in linking learning to the ports of call. Reports that the port experiences are the most meaningful program element in developing a global perspective. Advocates the importance of moving from the domestic classroom to experiential, field-based opportunities.

227. Mooney, Carolyn J. "Study Finds Professors Are Still Teaching the Classics, Sometimes in New Ways." *The Chronicle of Higher Education* 38 (11) (November 6, 1991): A1, A22.

Presents selected results of a 1991 Modern Language Association survey that found that English professors still rely heavily on traditional texts. Including responses from 571 English professors on more than 350 campuses, the survey showed that texts in three widely taught courses — 19th century American literature, the 19th century British novel, and Renaissance literature — still emphasized standard canonical authors. Points out and explains, however, that at the same time, there have been some significant changes in how literature is taught by including new books, asking new questions, and using new teaching methods. Examines, also, some specific criticism by the National Association of Scholars of the survey's results and implications.

228.    Musil, Caryn McTighe, ed. *The Courage to Question: Women's Studies and Student Learning.* Washington, DC: Association of American Colleges, 1992. 213 pp.

Presents the research findings from a comprehensive three-year research project aimed at evaluation and assessment of women's studies and student learning, launched by the National Women's Studies Association and funded by the Fund for the Improvement of Postsecondary Education. Program participants defined learning goals in four areas (i.e., knowledge base, learning skills, feminist pedagogy, and personal growth), developed institutional and program specific assessment techniques, and reflected on eight guiding questions common to all programs. Includes separate chapters describing each program's self-study along with copies of assessment questionnaires. Concludes with a summary of key findings about student learning in women's studies. An executive summary, published separately by the Association of American Colleges, gives an overview of the project.

229.    Musil, Caryn McTighe, ed. *Students at the Center: Feminist Assessment.* Washington, DC: Association of American Colleges, 1992. 120 pp.

The last of three publications from *The Courage to Question*, a research project funded by the U.S. Department of Education's Fund for the Improvement of Postsecondary Education. Focuses on the process, the how, and the why of assessment in women's studies and student learning. Argues for assessment that features context-specific questions, a context-specific set of means for gathering responses, and the centrality of students in the process. Chapters written by seven members of the National Assessment Team focus on the conceptual shifts, techniques, and methodologies that emerged from the programs involved in the assessment project. Asks "What is feminist assessment?"; reviews innovative assessment designs; offers practical advice; gives examples from specific institutions. Appendices include sample questionnaires, directory of consultants, and a brief bibliography.

230. Price, Riley P., and others. "Student and Faculty Perceptions of Women's Content in the Curriculum." *Journal of Education for Social Work* 15 (3) (Fall 1979): 51-57.

Reports survey data on the differences in perceptions among various groups of male and female students and faculty of content related to women in a school of social work. Finds the content on women generally to be inadequate, although faculty tend to consider the content they taught on women as adequate. Data from a content analysis of course outlines and bibliographies reveal very little content about women's concerns and issues, and very little concerning contemporary change in women's roles. Recommendations for curricular modification are cited. Defines the methodology used to gather information (from a midwestern college of social work) and analyzes the implications for social work specifically and higher education generally.

231. Richardson, Richard C., Jr., and Elizabeth Fisk Skinner. "Adapting to Diversity: Organizational Influences on Student Achievement." *The Journal of Higher Education* 61 (5) (September/October 1990): 485-511.

Explores the notion of institutional adaptation to the fact of increasing multicultural diversity (e.g., student demographics and curricular change) rather than student adaptation to a set of rigid institutional protocols. Discusses the tension between maintaining high standards of achievement/academic rigor and increasing institutional diversity; defends the fact that these two goals are not necessarily mutually exclusive. Presents and analyzes ten case studies of successful institutions — some highly selective and some with open access — and the general implications for curricular development. Emphasizes, ultimately, the coordination of a wide variety of institutional strategies designed to simultaneously focus on achievement and diversity. Describes a model of institutional adaptation to student diversity. Shows sensitivity to the unintended consequences of initiatives designed to enhance quality.

232.    Smythe, Mary-Jeanette, Sandy Nickel, and Anne Carman. "A Survey of Introductory Women Studies Courses." *Journal of the National Association for Women Deans, Administrators, and Counselors* 43 (4) (Summer 1980): 19-25.

Presents the results of a nationwide survey of women's studies programs. Focuses on introductory courses and examines trends in content and educational practices. Puts into perspective both the types of institutions most amenable to initiating and nurturing such programs and the overall pattern of development. Summarizes institution and program profiles, course orientation and content, and instructional strategies and materials. Respondents cite a multi-disciplinary study of women as the major thrust in content, and contemporary issues as the content area of greatest importance. Discussion led as the primary instructional strategy. Little agreement was found on the primary instructional materials. Summarizes both immediate status (1980) and the healthy prognosis for continued development.

233.    Zinsser, Judith P. *History and Feminism: A Glass Half Full.* New York: Twayne Publishers, 1993. 204 pp.

Presents an assessment of feminist impact on the discipline of history. Assesses changes in traditional (men's) history and women's history as the result of feminist inquiry. Reviews the impact of feminism in academic training, employment, and promotion in the field. Chapter 6 overviews changes in college courses, graduate programs, and publications over the past two decades. Finds that an androcentric perspective continues to dominate the teaching of history, and that even with changes in awareness, curriculum, and women's involvement, women's history still occupies a marginal place in the academy. Serves as one of the inaugural volumes in the series *Impact of Feminism on the Arts and Sciences* by Twayne Publishers. The series addresses questions such as which disciplines have been changed as a result of feminism and how.

# POLITICAL
# CORRECTNESS

"Political correctness" entered the educational lexicon near the end of the 1980s. Originally used rather self-deprecatingly by those advocating a range of reforms in higher education, the term has pejorated as the decibel level over its implication for higher education has risen in the volatile 1990s. The term has, in fact, come to symbolize to many the core around which the majority of issues about how colleges and universities should conduct their business has coalesced.

"Political correctness" most probably has contextually subtle distinctions in meaning. Generally, however, and for higher education, specifically, the term implies a response — whether personal or institutional — that is deemed appropriate based not on the inherent merits of an issue at stake but, rather, on extraneous considerations. These external factors are considered political, that is, characterized mainly by the power of numbers and expanded group influence: usually translated, this refers to minorities and women.

Inside the academy the commonly named "traditionalists" oppose campus decisions made for reasons other than what they deem as established academic merit or scholarly integrity. The newly empowered reformists counter that they deserve greater inclusion and argue that political power has served mainly to get them noticed; to them, to denigrate the intellectual contributions throughout history of women and minorities is abhorrent, a ploy used by the entrenched traditionalists who represent a formidable political power themselves: overwhelmingly white, Eurocentric males who have controlled and shaped the status quo for centuries.

In many ways, the appearance of the term and the polarizing effect that it often implies were inevitable. Even a cursory review of the literature — and only a layman's working knowledge of the history — of America from the early 1960s to the late 1980s shows the steady social, intellectual, and ideological growth that would lead to such harsh current contentiousness: for example, the victories of the civil-rights movement, "women's liberation," the many personal and cultural schisms produced by the Vietnam War, multiculturalism, black studies, women's studies, the implications of immigration policies, minority-student centers, affirmative action, "reverse discrimination," the notion of racial differences in intellect, ethnic pride, and the issue of freedom of speech vs. "hate-speech" codes. Seen as issues, these individually and collectively have come to affect a huge proportion of our population and seem to compel the taking of sides.

Since the late 1980s, the literature that is pertinent here centers around those issues that radiate from the terms and most clearly have an impact on the academy. In the largest sense, most who write on political correctness align themselves with one of the two previously mentioned groups: either the traditionalists — those who champion the centrality of accepted "traditional" intellectual and academic values — or the reformists — those who disdain what they see as the prevailing "Eurocentric," white-male-oriented tendency to exclude others' viewpoints and to assume that campus and curricular change must necessarily threaten academic integrity. And in the current climate of, among other campus realities, tight dwindling financial support, the sharp differences involved are exacerbated by the fact that many see eventual outcomes as the product of a serious zero-sum game: that is, for every course on, say, Native American literary tradition that is added, the traditionalist see a course on Twain or Faulkner lost. Conversely, every unchallenged, traditional course on, say, Locke and Kant that remains intact helps ensure that no new course on African philosophies will enter the curriculum.

For some, however, the stakes involved seem more subtle though equally important. For example, there are those who feel that the loud volume of the political-correctness debate serves as a convenient, high-profile vehicle for venting frustrations and dissatisfactions about higher education in general. For many of these scholars, the real problems of serious discussion on curricular inclusion, minority hiring, and true incidents of bias and harassment are relegated to a second tier of importance, too frequently lost beneath those instances that grab headlines. For these writers, the call usually is for a toning down of the volume and a commitment to dealing more thoughtfully with those underlying issues that, ultimately, will decide the direction of higher education in the twenty-first century.

Regardless of individual perceptions of the significance of the political-correctness debate, the literature of the last few years indicates that it is a serious, escalating issue that will take increasing amounts of academic time, energy, and resources to resolve, if resolution is, in fact, the appropriate goal. Some writers see no real chance for "resolution" because the battle lines are so distinct and the opinions emanate from such fundamentally differing concepts of what the academy is and where it is to go. In this paradigm, writers deal frequently with the necessity of working diligently, not for ultimate solutions, but for a continuing series of most-reasonable compromises.

Adding to the intensity of the debate are the voices of an increasing number of people outside higher education. Writers such as journalist George Will (no. 65) have taken the issues surrounding multiculturalism and political correctness past campus boundaries and into the public realm. Such dialogue tends to emphasize both the wide impact of the issues involved — freedom of speech, minority rights, and traditional family values crowd headlines almost everyday — and a growing impatience by outside constituencies for higher education to quit its internal squabbling and get about the business of educating. This ever-broadening base of people offering their perspectives tends to turn up the intensity of the already-bright spotlight on criticism of the academy.

At the same time, a number of writers labor at putting the political correctness debate in what they feel is a more realistic perspective. These writers often emphasize that not much has really changed in the academy: course offerings remain overwhelmingly as they were ten or fifteen years ago, and regardless of the rhetoric, colleges and universities go about their business with great degrees of regularity and with an almost surprising level of general public confidence  and increasing numbers of applicants. The implication is that higher education must, overall, be doing a lot more that is good and right than is bad or wrong. Critics of such a stance, however, argue that this is just another example of the complacency and negative inertia that hold back both social and intellectual progress on our nation's campuses.

Most writers agree that final results generated from the intense differences over political correctness should come from within the academy. After all, faculty determine curricula and graduation requirements because they are perceived as more qualified than, for example, trustees or legislators. The increasing range and intensity of debate about the implications of political correctness, however, serve notice that it is an issue that will not disappear, that it will have both immediate and long-range effects on higher education, and that more and more individuals feel compelled to join the dialogue.

## Political Correctness

234. Appleby, Joyce. "Recovering America's Historic Diversity: Beyond Exceptionalism." *The Journal of American History* 79 (2) (September 1992): 419-431.

Describes the growth of early American *exceptionalism*: a projection by others onto a nation — in this case, America — of supposedly exceptional qualities that are envied in relation to those of other, less-fortunate nations. Asserts that although this perception offered eighteenth-century Americans a singular collective identity, it today is America's own form of Eurocentrism. Feels that a continuing concept of American exceptionalism presents a powerful barrier to appreciating our inherent diversity. Discusses how exceptionalism created a national identity for the revolutionary generation and then examines how that identity hindered other ways of interpreting our national meaning. Deplores the Whiggish tendency to impress current values and norms onto the past and asserts that searching out and understanding those aspects of the American past that do not fit into the exceptionalist concept will require new levels of intellectual and analytical rigor.

235. Aufderheide, Patricia, ed. *Beyond P.C.: Toward a Politics of Understanding*. Saint Paul, MN: Graywolf Press, 1992. 239 pp.

Presents a series of point/counterpoint arguments concerning the current political-correctness debate. Included, for example, in the attack on P.C. are George F. Will (on literary politics), historian C. Vann Woodward (on freedom and the universities), and Mortimer J. Adler (on multiculturalism, transculturalism, and the great books). Included, for example, in the counterattack are Ruth Perry (on a short history of the term "politically correct"), Jon Wiener (on clarifying what actually happened at Harvard, a rebuttal to Dinesh D'Souza's charges in *Illiberal Education*), and Katharine T. Bartlett (on the power of P.C. critics). Also includes essays of personal experience, essays on moving beyond the current debate, and shares reflections from various sources (e.g., George Bush to Elizabeth Fox-Genovese).

236.    Beckwith, Francis, J., and Michael E. Bauman, eds. *Are You Politically Correct?: Debating America's Cultural Standards*. Buffalo, NY: Prometheus Books, 1993. 266 pp.

Divides chapters into five parts and a conclusion (proposals by Dinesh D'Souza): (1) the media and political correctness (a comprehensive definition of political correctness and rebuttal of the charge that campuses are besieged by the new P.C. radicals); (2) freedom of expression on campus (opposing views by Stanley Fish and Chester E. Finn, Jr.); (3) cultural diversity, the politics of race and sex on campus, and the western intellectual tradition (e.g., the challenge of diversity and multicultural education, new assaults on the curriculum, the value of the canon, and a Harvard University address by Allan Bloom); (4) multiculturalism and public education; and (5) quotas and campus diversity (opposing views by Stephen S. Weiner and William R. Beer on the responsibilities of accrediting bodies). Ends with the final chapter of Dinesh D'Souza's *Illiberal Education: The Politics of Race and Sex on Campus*.

237.    Berman, Paul. "Introduction: The Debate and Its Origins." In *Debating P.C.: The Controversy over Political Correctness on College Campuses*, edited by Paul Berman, 1-26. New York: Dell Publishing, 1992.

Traces in his introduction the origin and development of the political-correctness debate and puts the current discussions in context by analyzing historical antecedents in America and identifying international comparisons, especially from France. Then collects and divides a collection of essays into six parts: (1) debating political correctness (an interview with Dinesh D'Souza, author of *Illiberal Education*; the Modern Language Association [MLA], presidential address, 1990; the MLA in Chicago; controversy at the university level; and the media's distortion of the political-correctness debate); (2) politics and the canon (a defense of the canon's value, the politics of knowledge, the relativity and arbitrary quality of a canon, and a look at the problematic essentials of the debate, e.g., why do we read?); (3) free speech and speech codes (the problem with campus codes, the freedom of hate speech, and a defense of codes); (4) the Texas shoot-out (the controversy at the University of Texas, Austin (UT), including a statement from the UT Black Faculty Caucus, a defense of the traditional curriculum, and an attack on the critics of attempts to democratize the curriculum); (5) the public schools (on multiculturalism); and (6) diverse views (disparate looks at the current status of the debate and the inherent challenges to the academy).

238.　Beyer, Landon E. "The Curriculum, Social Context, and 'Political Correctness'." *The Journal of General Education* 43 (1) (1994):1-31.

Begins with an exploration of the term *political correctness* and the associated language (e.g., military terminology) used by some in the debates. Focuses on the epistemological underpinnings of the curriculum and the way these debates raise fundamental questions about values and principles. Examines the idea that the criteria for inclusion and exclusion of knowledge are not only intellectual but also political and ideological. Questions the impact of budgetary constraints, publishers, and educational activities at the college and secondary school level on change, or lack thereof, in curricula. Provides justifications, from both demography and critical analyses, for generating a more multicultural curriculum. Includes reflections on the writings and arguments of various participants (e.g., Cheney, D'Souza,

Kimball, Bloom, and Hirsch) in the debate. Advances that a common theme runs through the conservatives' critique of political correctness: truth is immutable, transcendent, and not connected to historical, social, political, or ideological contexts. Concludes with the importance of revealing the political nature of the traditionalists and the value-ladenness associated with allegedly objective curricula, activities, and writings.

239.     Bronwich, David. *Politics by Other Means: Higher Education and Group Thinking*. New Haven, CT: Yale University Press, 1992. 257 pp.

Draws a distinction between politics and education. Assesses the strengths and weaknesses of the political/ educational, liberal/traditional controversy. Also includes chapters on the new fundamentalists; moral education during Reagan's 1980s; the limits of institutional radicalism; reflection, morality, and tradition; and the specific case of literary study. Includes a general conclusion and extensive explanatory notes.

240.     Burd, Stephen. "Humanities Chief Assails Politicization of Classrooms." *The Chronicle of Higher Education* 39 (6) (September 30, 1992): A21-A22.

Summarizes a report — *Telling the Truth* — by then-chairman of the National Endowment for the Humanities, Lynne V. Cheney. Presents her basic thesis that the aim of higher education has moved from the pursuit of truth to political transformation — of both students and society. Also notes that she calls for an increasing involvement by alumni groups and especially by trustees, who, she says, should use their influence and authority to help preserve academic freedom. States her belief that universities and colleges should return to a more traditional core curriculum and maintain high academic standards. Identifies both defenders and critics of Cheney's ideas and presents some of their conflicting arguments.

241.   Collins, Huntly. "PC and the Press." *Change* 24 (1) (January/February 1992): 12-16.

Asserts that the influence of political correctness on college campuses has been highly exaggerated, thus distorting the state of affairs in American higher education. Cites the mainstream media's tendency to be alarmist when, for example, deconstructionism has been heatedly controversial at only the highly selective private schools and the Ivys and Western culture, including science and technology, is still at the curricular core. Calls for a clear-eyed analysis of legitimate differences of opinion without the reactionary tendency to lump these differences into reductive categories of correctness.

242.   Daniels, Lee A. "Diversity, Correctness, and Campus Life: A Closer Look." *Change* 23 (5) (September/October 1991): 16-20.

Feels that the political-correctness debate may be less about the inherent attributes of political correctness and more about other dissatisfactions with higher education. Feels, thus, that political correctness has become merely a convenient vehicle for venting these other frustrations. Wants colleges and universities to deal honestly and openly with the real problems — curricular inclusion, minority hiring and promotion, serious incidents of bias and harassment, for example — and not settle for the headlines that can be easily grabbed by superficial condemnations of abstract political correctness and by the appearance of being diverse.

243.   Dickie, Margaret M. "PC, PR and Research in the '90s." *The University of Georgia Research Reporter* 22 (2) (November 1992): 11-13.

Notes that the political-correctness movement is not restricted to the humanities. Even in the sciences, political correctness always has been more or less present. Gives governmental and industrial examples of forces that define much of the nature of higher educational research. Describes the negative conservative effect of political correctness on scientific research, specifically. Examines some of the positive, as well as the negative, aspects of political correctness influence in the political correctness-versus-intellectual freedom debate. Describes the need for higher education to promote itself and to create a more inclusive scholarly community that transcends some of the ill effects of overspecialization and, at the same time, takes best advantage of the academy's inherent multicultural environment.

244.    D'Souza, Dinesh. *Illiberal Education: The Politics of Race and Sex on Campus.* New York: The Free Press, 1991. 319 pp.

Condemns much of the political correctness/multicultural movement as it has been manifested on a number of prominent campuses. After a general analysis of what he terms the victim's revolution on campus, looks specifically at incidents at six major universities: the admissions policy at the University of California, Berkeley; multiculturalism at Stanford; the roots of protest at Harvard; racial incidents at the University of Michigan; what he sees as the subversion of academic standards at Duke; and the teaching of race and gender at Harvard. Has a concluding chapter that includes recommendations for changes and courses of action.

245.    Frye, Marilyn. "Getting It Right." *Signs: Journal of Women in Culture and Society* 17(4) (Summer 1992): 781-93.

Defines the evolution of the terms *politically correct* and *politically incorrect* and then redefines ideally the former. Looks at politics in both our general culture and the academy. Delineates important distinctions among such key terms as *affirmative action* (defined mainly as a less-than successful strategy that allows the majority in power to assimilate token minorities who most resemble the entrenched structure), *curriculum integration* (the curricular version of affirmative action), and *multiculturalism* (the true affirmation of plurality). Argues for an academy based on a politics of knowledge emphasized by communal and disciplinary separation, creation, and autonomy and by a minimization of adversarial, coercive, or reformist engagement.

246.   Gates, Henry Louis, Jr. "Whose Canon is it, Anyway?" In *Debating P.C.: The Controversy Over Political Correctness on College Campuses*, edited by Paul Berman, 190-200. New York: Dell Publishing, 1992.

Criticizes traditionalists like William Bennett and Allan Bloom as symbols of what he sees as a nostalgic return to an antebellum aesthetic position predicated on the concepts that men were men and men were white, scholar-critics were white men, and women and people of color were voiceless, faceless servants and laborers. Defends the need to reform and expand core curricula to include the African, Asian, and Middle Eastern traditions, thus helping to prepare students for their roles as world citizens who would be educated through a truly human notion of the humanities, rather than as guardians of white male culture. Discusses the concept of a literary canon and the difficulty in balancing, for example, an anthology of African-American literature between those who would argue that black literature can have no canon or masterpieces, and those who wonder why anyone wants to establish the existence of any canon.

247.   Gless, Darryl J., and Barbara Herrnstein Smith, eds. *The Politics of Liberal Education*. Durham, NC: Duke University Press, 1992. 305 pp.

With two exceptions, presents versions of papers from the 1988 conference "Liberal Arts Education in the Late Twentieth Century: Emerging Conditions, Responsive Practices," held at Duke University and the University of North Carolina. Responds to traditionalists' attacks on the direction of reform in contemporary humanities teaching. Includes essays on, for example, the convergence of democracy, technology, theory, and the university curriculum; canon formation and the African-American tradition; pedagogy in the context of an antihomophobic project; the academy and the public; praise for the cultural left; and the need to reject what is perceived as the nostalgia of much traditionalist argument and, rather, to enfold present arguments and discontents into teaching practice and curricular direction.

248.  Heller, Scott. "'Frame-up' of Multicultural Movement Dissected by Scholars and Journalists." *The Chronicle of Higher Education* 28 (14) (November 27, 1991): A15-A16.

Presents details of a University of Michigan conference ("The PC Frame-up: What's Behind the Attack?") of journalists, scholars, and media critics. Notes that the conference included a few members of those critical of the direction of campus intellectual life, but was largely comprised of those who support scholarly and curricular change and who argue that these efforts have been consistently misrepresented. Presents an excellent short analysis of the arguments and rationales of some of the most visible proponents of the political-correctness/multicultural agenda.

249.  Hogan, Patrick Colm. "Mo' Better Canons: What's Wrong and What's Right about Mandatory Diversity." *College English* 54 (2) (February 1992): 182-192.

Analyzes both sides in the political correctness/ multicultural debates, focusing on the implications for a comparative-literature curriculum. Thoughtfully sides with the need to have a more diverse, inclusive curriculum but not without dealing carefully with all cogent arguments to the contrary. Argues of the need to reduce Western ignorance of both non-Western traditions and Western minority traditions and for a recognition that the status quo inherently perpetuates a subtle, but pervasive, structural and institutional discrimination that is often difficult to perceive. Asserts, ultimately, that cross-cultural literary study is very desirable on intellectual, aesthetic, and ethical grounds. Attempts to refute carefully any arguments to the contrary.

250.     Howe, Irving. "The Value of the Canon." In *Debating P.C.: The Controversy Over Political Correctness on College Campuses*, edited by Paul Berman, 153-171. New York: Dell Publishing, 1992.

Without vindicating socialism or Marxism, disputes the claim that the politically correct antitraditionalists speak from a left, let alone a Marxist, point of view. Characterizes the ferment on campus today as a curious mixture of American populist sentiment and French critical theory. Defends the traditional canon by countering arguments for injecting political and ideological components into curricular choices. Looks at the history of the debate and presents rebuttals to, or answers for, the most-often-quoted arguments and questions posed by multicultural proponents.

251.     Leatherman, Courtney. "AAUP Statement on the 'Political Correctness' Debate Causes a Furor." *The Chronicle of Higher Education* 38 (15) (December 4, 1991): A23-A24.

Describes the dissension inside the American Association of University Professors over an *ad hoc*, four-member committee's statement on the political-correctness controversy. Highlights the confusion within an even older established organization concerning the academic versus political implications of this subject.

252.     Lewis, Florence C. "A Report from the PC Front." *The College Board Review* 161 (Fall 1991): 2-7.

Cautions, first, that we must be aware that *politics* and *correctness* are not the same thing: the former connoting that which, essentially, is shrewd, practical, cunning, and crafty, and the latter connoting that which is straight, right, and geared toward removing error. Argues, thus, that political correctness is often closer to political corruption for the obvious reason that power corrupts even when power is exchanged. Argues, further, that political correctness generated out of a base or too-personal motive can lead to narrow, negative curricular changes, not to changes that

reflect and integrate the best that a diverse, multicultural
society has to offer.

253.    Magner, Denise K. "Gathering to Assess Battle Against
        'Political Correctness,' Scholars Look for New Ways to Resist
        'Illiberal Radicals'." *The Chronicle of Higher Education* 38 (10)
        (October 30, 1991): A17-A18.

        Presents details of the third National Association of
        Scholars (NAS) conference. Notes that the NAS response was
        to political correctness and multiculturalism as perceived
        threats: academe is still controlled by those perceived as
        illiberal radicals who pursue social agendas. Describes the
        movement of NAS from a group who earlier considered
        themselves as political and intellectual conservatives fighting
        against a hostile and increasingly radical campus
        environment to a group who are seeking practical strategies
        to resist what they see as the multiple threats of diversity and
        multiculturalism. Also describes a new group, Teachers for
        a Democratic Culture, that hopes to counter what is
        perceived as distortions by the NAS.

254.    Schultz, Debra L., and others. *To Reclaim a Legacy of Diversity:
        Analyzing 'Political Correctness' Debates in Higher Education.*
        Edited by Susan A. Hallgarth. New York: National Council
        for Research on Women, 1993. 74 pp.

        Serves both as a report on the status of the political-
        correctness phenomenon on campus and as a resource guide
        to then-current material to aid in expanding the networks of
        those engaged in women's studies and feminist research.
        Includes chapters on the definition of PC, media coverage,
        conservative attacks on change in the academy, liberal
        responses to backlash, declining dollars to higher education,
        and a look at campus realities that imply necessary change.
        Also includes a selected bibliography and eight appendices:
        (1) selected chronology of media coverage, (2) activist
        networks of student newspapers on campuses, (3)
        statements on *political correctness*, (4) National Endowment
        for the Humanities funding, (5) representation of people of

color and women on campus, (6) National Council for Research on Women member centers, (7) selected guides and resources for integrating women of color into the curriculum, and (8) other resources for change in higher education.

255. Scott, Joan Wallach. "The Campaign Against Political Correctness: What's Really at Stake?" *Change* 23 (6) (November/December 1991): 30-43.

Presents a comprehensive view of the implications of the political-correctness controversy. Describes the traditionalists (who, she feels, tap into a long-standing American tendency to distrust intellectuals) as paranoid (us, the pure keepers of the flames, versus them, aggressive and destructive), as self-assured, ill informed imposters, and as fetishists who have used the concept of tradition (the embodiment of taste, culture, and cumulative wisdom) for the claim to white male privilege they want to preserve. Explores the strain of anti-intellectualism that she feels has been clearly around since the 1950s and is relevant in today's attitudes. Explores, also, the necessity of redefining the notion of community and of the importance of not always seeking consensus.

256. Thibodaux, David. *Political Correctness: The Cloning of the American Mind.* Lafayette, LA: Huntington House Publishers, 1992. 212 pp.

Presents a comprehensive analysis of the impact of political correctness on higher education: definition and background; an in-depth look at the components of multiculturalism, Afrocentrism, genderism, and political-correctness terrorism; suggestions for ways to counter the negative effects of political correctness; interviews with administrators and faculty who tend to buttress his arguments; and a short, general conclusion.

257. Trachtenberg, Stephen Joel. "Political Correctness: Can It Ever Be Politically Incorrect?" *The College Board Review* 165 (Early Winter 1992-93): 6-11.

Gives an account of how political correctness began, along with observations from his days at Columbia University. Notes that the perspective of the world as holding multiple traditions combined with the counterculture movement of the 1960s and 1970s to break the curriculum from its Judeo-Christian roots. Advances that much of political correctness stems from (1) loss of confidence in our own traditions, (2) difficulty reconciling rapid change in ethnic and socioeconomic patterns, and (3) acceptance of the notion that our Western traditions were connected to our economic and military strength. Asserts that political correctness is neither all right nor wrong, but is an avenue to self-scrutiny. Suggests that new student populations with high levels of computer and technological literacy will require more than the inclusion of new texts and underrepresented perspectives. Provides an illustration of how future faculty will need to move among traditional scholarship, emerging perspectives, and contemporary information technology to connect with students.

258.     Treichler, Paula A., Cheris Kramarae, and Beth Stafford, eds. *For Alma Mater: Theory and Practice in Feminist Scholarship.* Urbana, IL: University of Illinois Press, 1985. 450 pp.

Among other essays, includes difference and continuity in feminist criticism, feminism and critical theory, the maturing of Chicana poetry in the 1980s, feminism in linguistics, interdisciplinary studies and a feminist community, refusing the legacy of institutional racism and sexism, recent directions in women's history, failures of androcentric studies of women's education in the third world, the arcane nature of men and their institutions, resources for the Chicana feminist scholar, and the implications of being a feminist academic. Also includes an assessment of current library research in women's studies.

# GUIDE TO RESOURCES:
# BIBLIOGRAPHIES AND REFERENCE BOOKS

The annotations presented in previous sections address multiculturalism's integration and transformation of the curricula of higher education; however, that is but one dimension of multicultural change in the academy. This chapter presents books and articles that broadly address multiculturalism and higher education—the changes in clientele, teaching, research, and the culture of higher education. Included are directories, bibliographies, guides and indices covering a wide variety of issues.

259.    Afro-American Studies and Research Program, University of Illinois, Urbana; Illinois Council for Black Studies; and the National Council for Black Studies. *Guide to Scholarly Journals in Black Studies*. Chicago: Peoples College Press, 1981. 71 pp.

   Presents an early attempt to catalogue the growing number of professional journals on black studies. Arranges these journals in alphabetical order and also provides (1) background information, such as publisher, editors, and date founded; (2) general information on the content of the journal, such as the types of material accepted and the subject range; (3) submission and subscription information. Includes a comprehensive introduction with bibliography and both topical and name indexes.

260.    Ariel, Joan. *Building Women's Studies Collections: A Resource Guide*. Middletown, CT: CHOICE bibliographical essay series (8), American Library Association, 1987. 48 pp.

   Includes sections on, for example, resources for initial collections, review media, feminist publishers, publishers with women's studies catalogs or lists, microform and manuscript sources and collections, databases and data sets, dissertations, curriculum and program materials, bookdealers, miscellaneous resources, and a selected bibliography.

261.  Aguirre, Adalberto, Jr., and Ruben O. Martinez. *Chicanos in Higher Education: Issues and Dilemmas for the 21st Century.* ASHE-ERIC Higher Education Report No. 3. Washington, DC: The George Washington University, School of Education and Human Development, 1993. 108 pp.

Includes sections on (1) the education of Chicanos (e.g., demographic changes and the postsecondary context), (2) Chicanos' access to higher education (e.g., student affirmative action and the development of Chicano studies), (3) the participation of Chicanos in higher education (e.g., the undergraduate experience and trends), (4) Chicano faculty in higher education (e.g., institutional stratification and dilemmas), and (5) the education of Chicanos in the 21st century (e.g., context and educational policy). Includes a summary of each section and an extensive list of references.

262.  Atkinson, Steven D., and Judith Hudson, eds. *Women Online: Research in Women's Studies Using Online Databases.* New York: The Haworth Press, 1990. 420 pp.

Divides the database resources into 16 typical categories: (1) humanities, (2) social and behavioral sciences, (3) biomedicine, (4) women's issues and online legal research, (5) business, (6) information about women in reference databases, (7) news and popular databases, (8) feminist perspectives through cited reference searching, (9) women in the national online bibliographic database, (10) women in nonbibliographic databases, (11) lesbians, (12) women of color, (13) women in developing countries, (14) women's studies curriculum materials, (15) sports, and (16) government. Also includes a database matrix.

263.  Ballou, Patricia K. *Women: A Bibliography of Bibliographies.* 2nd ed. Boston: G.K. Holland Co., 1986. 268 pp.

Concerned primarily with bibliographies about women or topics traditionally associated with women. Along with the subcategories of higher education and women's studies, includes an extensive list of topical subjects (e.g., history, literature, mass media and popular culture, fine arts, religion, economics, political science, and sociology) and sections based on the general and the interdisciplinary, publications of one type or format, and geographical subjects. Also indexed by name, title, and subject.

264.   Barrett, Jacquline, ed. *Encyclopedia of Women's Associations Worldwide*. London: Gale Research International, Ltd., 1993. 471 pp.

Provides access to associations and related nonprofit, national, and multinational organizations worldwide. Organizes the list by continent and country. Gives founding dates, number of staff, language, and a brief description of the organization, along with publications. Also presents the organizations in a useful topical index (e.g., African-American, arts, education, women's studies, and sororities).

265.   Brownmiller, Sara, and Ruth Dickstein. *An Index to Women's Studies Anthologies: Research Across the Disciplines, 1980-84*. New York: G.K. Hall and Co., 1994. 494 pp.

Provides access to the contents of almost 500 anthologies, covering all disciplines, published between 1980 and 1984 that have as a focus women and women's issues. Is divided into 5 sections: (1) alphabetical listing of anthologies with complete bibliographic information and table of contents; (2) subject index grouping the books into 36 broad categories; (3) editor index with book entry number; (4) author index with book entry number and chapter letter; and (5) keyword index, composing one-half of the book. Includes in subject headings, for example, feminist theory, women's studies, education, history, area studies, and international studies.

266.   Carnegie Foundation for the Advancement of Teaching. *Tribal Colleges: Shaping the Future of Native America*. Princeton,

NJ: The Carnegie Foundation for the Advancement of Teaching, 1989.

Presents a critique of a two-year study and visits to seven tribal colleges. Looks at a diverse range of topics, from educational philosophy and curriculum to student profiles and communal interaction. Includes a foreword by Ernest L. Boyer and six chapters: (1) a new era for tribal colleges, (2) a historical perspective, (3) tribal colleges as survivors, (4) tribal colleges in the context of the larger Native American movement, (5) colleges that build communities, and (6) ten recommendations for ensuring the growth and quality of Native-American education and tribal colleges.

267.    Carter, Sarah, and Maureen Ritchie. *Women's Studies: A Guide to Information Sources*. London: Mansell Publishing Limited, 1990. 278 pp.

Includes information divided into three main parts: (1) general material (reference sources, biographical information, and women's studies), (2) women in the world (international perspectives, Africa, Asia and the Pacific, Australia and New Zealand, Europe, Latin America and the Caribbean, the Middle East, and North America), and (3) special subjects (e.g., the arts and media; black women; education; history; science, mathematics, and technology; spirituality, mythology, and religion; and women in the labor force). Also includes a postscript on men's studies.

268.    Davis, Lenwood G., and George Hill. *A Bibliographical Guide to Black Studies Programs in the United States*. Westport, CT: Greenwood Press, 1985. 120 pp.

Presents a variety of sources on black studies programs, including 79 major books and pamphlets; 72 books on general works, many discussing black students on white university campuses and their demands for black studies; more than 68 dissertations (the earliest is 1943); and more than 500 articles. Also includes a comprehensive index of authors, joint authors, and editors, all numbered by individual entry.

269.    De La Rosa, Denise and Carlyle E. Maw. *Hispanic Education: A Statistical Portrait 1990*. Washington, DC: National Council of La Raza, 1990. 114 pp.

Along with chapters on K-12 Hispanic students and elementary and secondary school teachers and administrators, includes a statistical chapter on postsecondary education (e.g., SAT scores, continuity of enrollment, enrollment by type of institution, and degrees conferred). Presents separate chapters on adult/young-adult Hispanics and on policy implications and recommendations. Also includes at the end of each chapter a section on statistical implications.

270.    Dost, Jeanne, ed. *Women Studies Bibliography: Kerr Library Collection*. Corvallis, OR: Women Studies Program, Oregon State University, 1983. 133 pp.

Presents a first attempt to identify all publications on women based in the Kerr Library through the spring of 1982 at Oregon State University. Includes more than four pages related specifically to education. Also includes a broad selection of other disciplines and topics, ranging from, for example, anthropology and art to fiction and foreign countries to law/politics, psychology, science, sex roles, sports, and women's studies.

271.    Escobedo, Theresa Herrera, ed. *Education and Chicanos: Issues and Research*. No. 8. Los Angeles: University of California, Spanish Speaking Mental Health Research Center, 1981. 220 pp.

Includes chapters addressing sociocultural approach for educational research and research in bilingual/bicultural educational settings. Three chapters address higher education: (1) achieving equity through the inclusion and retention of Hispanic academics, (2) increasing opportunities for minorities and women in research, and (3) examining the coping behaviors of Anglos and Mexican-American university students.

272.    Franzosa, Susan D. and Karen A. Mazza. *Integrating Women's Studies into the Curriculum: An Annotated Bibliography.* Westport, CT: Greenwood Press, 1984. 100 pp.

Arranges entries into nine categories: (1) bibliographic studies and resource guides, (2) issues and perspectives on the integration of women's studies, (3) literary studies and writing, (4) science and technology, (5) quantitative reasoning, (6) historical perspectives, (7) fine arts, (8) philosophic and theological perspectives, and (9) social science perspectives. Further divides categories 3-9 into subcategories, including women in the profession, reconceptualizaing the discipline, thematic studies, and curriculum strategies. Also includes a directory of sources (e.g., American Anthropological Association, American Educational Research Association, Modern Language Association, and the Wellesley College Center for Research on Women).

273.    Gilbert, V.F., and D.S. Tatla. *Women's Studies: A Bibliography of Dissertations 1870-1982.* New York: Basil Blackwell Inc., 1985. 496 pp.

Comprehensive list of theses and dissertations on women's studies presented at British Canadian, Irish, and North American universities up to, and including, 1982. Along with the bibliography, explains the rationale for coverage, and the method of preparation. Also includes a checklist of bibliographical and reference sources and an index.

274.    Glazer, Judith S., Estela M. Bensimon, and Barbara K. Townsend. *Women in Higher Education: A Feminist Perspective.* ASHE Reader Series. Needham Heights, MA: Ginn Press, 1993. 600 pp.

Includes 40 articles compiled to examine women's place in the academy. Begins with a prologue written by the editors. Notes that higher education as a field of study has been more reticent than the liberal arts to examine women as contributors and shapers of the academy. Divides the articles into four major content areas: (1) theoretical and research perspectives (e.g., Gilligan's "Woman's Place in Man's Life Cycle," Acker's "Hierarchies, Jobs, and Bodies: A Theory of Gendered Organizations"); (2) historical, social, professional, and institutional context (e.g., Sandler's "The Campus Climate Revisited: Chilly for Women Faculty, Administrators, and Graduate Students"); (3) women in academe: students, faculty, administrators, and trustees (e.g., hooks' "black and female: reflections on graduate school"); and (4) transformation of knowledge: curricular change and feminist pedagogy (e.g., Higginbotham's "Designing an Inclusive Curriculum: Bringing All Women into the Core"). Concludes with a selective bibliography, including additional reading suggestions in the four major areas.

275. Gutierrez, Ginny, and Ward Morehouse, eds. *International Studies Funding and Resources Book: The Education Interface Guide to Sources of Support for International Education*. 5th ed. New York: The Apex Press, 1990.

Presents profiles and sources of funding and resources for international education, including government agencies; United States and foreign; and private or nongovernmental organizations, such as foundations, professional associations, and research groups. Includes a separate section on nationally funded resource centers in language, area, and international studies; area-studies associations; community world affairs organizations; and foreign governments and film distribution services. Also gives practical suggestions (e.g., how to write a grant proposal) and sources of information and help.

276. Harvey, William B. "Education in the Black Community." *Journal of Black Studies* 19 (2) (December 1988): 131-189.

Includes articles on schooling and socioeconomic advancement for black Americans, public policies and financial exigencies, black colleges twenty years later, 1965-1985, blacks in graduate and professional schools, and ideology in teacher education.

277. Hsia, Jayjia. *Asian Americans in Higher Education and at Work.* Hillsdale, NJ: Lawrence Erlbaum Associates, Inc., 1988. 238 pp.

Along with a section on education, occupation, and income, includes six other pertinent sections: (1) the implications of background and demographic factors; (2) Asian American abilities (e.g., admission test scores and graduate and professional studies); (3) academic and extracurricular achievements (e.g., English and mathematics proficiencies; differential achievement; extracurricular activities, honors, and awards; and changes over time); (4) aspirations, access, enrollment, major fields, and persistence; (5) higher education achievement; and (6) summary, conclusions, and recommendations. Includes an extensive list of references and both author and subject indexes.

278. Humphreys, Debra, ed. *Guide to Graduate Work in Women's Studies.* College Park, MD: National Women's Studies Association, 1991. 98 pp.

Presents an informational listing of graduate-level work in women's studies. Each alphabetical entry includes degrees offered, program structure and specific requirements, departments that encourage women's studies, number of graduate courses offered solely in women's studies, selected women's studies and related courses, courses that concentrate on race or sexual orientation, particular program strengths or emphases, women's studies core and affiliate faculty, and financial aid availability. Also includes indexes by both state and degree offered and a list of additional programs (from schools that either did not respond to the initial survey or have limited graduate offerings).

279. Jorgensen, Mary Anne, comp. *A Directory of Selected Research and Policy Centers Working on Women's Issues*. Fifth ed. Washington, DC: The Women's Research and Education Institute, 1989. 43 pp.

Along with entities not directly related to higher education, includes, for example, the Center for Women's Studies; Center for Advanced Feminist Studies; Feminist Studies Center; Higher Education Research Institute; Institute for Research on Women, Rutgers; Pembroke Center for Teaching and Research on Women; Smith College Project on Women and Social Change; Women's Studies Program and Policy Center; and Women's Studies Research Center. Includes for each entry the vital statistics (e.g., address, phone number, and contact person), the primary activities and particular areas of expertise. Also includes tabular formats for quick view of primary activities and research topics that are being pursued by each center. Has a final appendix that lists centers by three criteria: particular expertise on minority women, information on selected policy-relevant topics, and alphabetical state location.

280. Joyce, Donald Franklin, comp. *Blacks in the Humanities, 1750-1984: A Selected Annotated Bibliography*. New York: Greenwood Press, Inc., 1986. 209 pp.

Presents major published and unpublished sources in English about the contributions of black Americans in eleven disciplines — philosophy, religion, journalism, libraries and librarianship, folklore, linguistics, art, music, performing arts, literary criticism, and cultural and intellectual history — and in a general works category — general bibliographies, indexes, union lists, encyclopedias, biographical dictionaries, library catalogues, compilations and collections, classic organizational and institutional publications, and directories. Also includes subject and author-title indexes.

281. Kim, Hyung-chan, ed. *Asian American Studies: An Annotated Bibliography and Research Guide*. New York: Greenwood Press, 1989. 504 pp.

Begins with essays on (1) research in history and the social sciences as they relate to the Asian American experience and (2) on Pacific migration as defined by American historians and social theorists up to the 1960s. Then includes annotated bibliographies divided into two categories: historical perspectives (e.g.,culture, communication, and education; community and organizations; nativism, exclusion, and race relations; acculturation, assimilation, and identity; and local and regional history) and contemporary perspectives (e.g., education and language learning; population and demography; stereotypes, prejudice, and race relations; and Asian American women's studies). Also includes an introduction for each category and author and subject indexes.

282.    Lehmann, Stephen and Eva Sartori, eds. *Women's Studies in Western Europe: A Resource Guide.* Chicago: Association of College and Research Libraries, 1986. 129 pp.

Presents annotations of comparative works and lists of relevant organizations, archives, libraries, information centers, etc. in Western Europe. Includes essays on the state of women's publishing; women's studies; and collection development and women's heritage at the Fawcett Library, the oldest and largest library in Britain devoted entirely to the study of women. Also includes an appendix of American periodicals relevant to European women's studies.

283.    Lewis, Chris H. *Developing an Inclusive Curriculum: A Curriculum Guide for Multicultural Education.* Minneapolis: University of Minnesota, General College, 1990. ERIC, ED 326089.

Presents a bibliography that lists resources and provides a framework for developing teaching materials and approaches to multiculturalism across the curriculum. Lists items according to this arrangement: (1) general articles on multicultural education and (2) resources for teaching by (a) subject area, (b) cultural group, and (c) concept (e.g., class, power, ethnicity, and gender). Along with complete bibliographic information for each entry, includes descriptive annotations for some.

284. Loeb, Catherine R., Susan E. Searing, and Esther F. Stineman (with the assistance of Meredith J. Ross). *Women's Studies: A Recommended Core Bibliography 1980-85*. Littleton, CO: Libraries Unlimited, Inc., 1987. 538 pp.

Includes annotations of material covering a number of relevant categories of women's studies: anthropology, cross-cultural surveys, and international studies; art and material culture; autobiography, biography, diaries, memoirs, and letters; business, economics and labor; education and pedagogy; history; language and linguistics; law; literature; medicine, health, sexuality, and biology; politics and political theory; psychology; religion and philosophy; science, mathematics, and technology; sociology and social issues; sports; and women's movement and feminist theory. Also presents a look at available reference materials and current periodicals. Is indexed according to author, title, and subject.

285. Miller, Connie, and Corinna Treitel. *Feminist Research Methods: An Annotated Bibliography*. New York: Greenwood Press, 1991. 279 pp.

Begins with a concise summary of the influence of feminism on traditional research and cites some of the disappointments encountered in general while compiling this bibliography: specifically, and most common, that feminist research generally is no more accessible to those outside the specialty areas than traditional research. Includes works that describe how feminists practice research in ways different from other researchers. Includes chapters on sociology, anthropology, psychology, history, political science, economics, geography/architecture, and communication, along with short introductions to each.

286. Mitchell, Robert. *The Multicultural Student's Guide to Colleges: What Every African-American, Asian-American, Hispanic, and*

*Native American Applicant Needs to Know about America's Top Schools*. New York: The Noonday Press, 1993. 839 pp.

Examines the top colleges and universities in America according to a number of criteria, including the application process; financial aid opportunities; percentage of tenured and nontenured faculty who are African-American, Asian-American, Hispanic, and Native American; ethnic studies programs and courses; scholarships exclusively for students of color; percentages of male and female minority students; comments from current students about their school; and campus life, including student organizations and theme houses. Also presents basic factual information (e.g., address, pertinent phone numbers, tuition and room and board costs, retention rate of nonwhite students, student-to-faculty ratio, and notable nonwhite alumni. Gives a list of predominantly black colleges and universities and suggestions about choosing one.

287.    Nordquist, Joan, comp. *The Multicultural Education Debate in the University: A Bibliography*. Number 25 in "Contemporary Social Issues: A Bibliographic Series," Santa Cruz, CA: Reference and Research Services, 1992 (not annotated). 63 pp.

Includes sections that cover seven major areas: (1) the political correctness debate (books and articles), (2) the intellectual and political climate of the university (with selected critiques of Bloom's *The Closing of the American Mind*, D'Souza's *Illiberal Education*, Jacoby's *The Last Intellectuals*, Kimball's *Tenured Radicals*, and Sykes's *Profscam*, plus other related books and articles), (3) freedom of speech on the campus (books and articles), (4) multicultural education in the university (books and articles), (5) Eurocentrism in the curriculum with selected critiques of Amin's *Eurocentrism* and Bernal's *Black Athena*, plus other related books and articles, (6) women in the curriculum (books and articles), and (7) resources (organizations).

288. Nordquist, Joan, comp. *Feminist Theory: A Bibliography*, Social Theory: A Bibliographic Series No. 28. Santa Cruz, CA: Reference and Research Services, 1992. 76 pp.

Provides an introduction to literature about feminist theory. Primarily lists books beginning with the mid-1970s, although some articles and essays in books about feminist theory are included. Divided into three sections: general feminist theory, feminist theory in the social science disciplines, and feminist literary criticism. Of particular interest are the separate works listed for the disciplines of sociology, political science, anthropology, and history. Not annotated.

289. Olivas, Michael A., ed. *Latino College Students*. New York: Teachers College Press, Columbia University, 1986. 360 pp.

Includes essays divided into three major topical categories: (1) the transition from high school to college (e.g., the relationship of school outcomes, family background, and high school curriculum and Hispanic college choices), (2) Hispanic student achievement (e.g., research findings about the Latino science and engineering student and prediction of Hispanics' college achievement), and (3) economics and stratification (e.g., barriers to Chicana and Chicano progress and financial aid strategies).

290. Ramsey, Patricia G., Edwina Battle Void, and Leslie R. Williams. *Multicultural Education: A Source Book*. New York: Garland Publishing, Inc., 1989. 177 pp.

An annotated bibliography with chapter summaries describing multicultural education overall and specifically in primary and secondary settings. Includes five chapters: (1) the evolution of multicultural education: a sociopolitical perspective; (2) ethnic diversity and children's learning; (3) multicultural programs, curricula, and strategies; (4) multicultural teacher education; and (5) future directions in multicultural education. Discusses multiculturalism in the context of the intergroup education movement, the ethnic studies movement, and the evolution of cultural pluralism in the United States. Provides in chapter 4 a brief history of multicultural teacher education, NCATE standards for multicultural education, goals and guidelines for multicultural teacher education, and a summary of case studies in teacher education programs. Concludes with a call for commitment to educational equity, the principle avenue to incorporating multicultural perspectives in schools.

291.    Schmitz, Betty. *Integrating Women's Studies into the Curriculum: A Guide and Bibliography.* Old Westbury, NY: The Feminist Press, 1985. 192 pp.

Provides an overview of curriculum integration and its origins. Discusses project design, implementation, and evaluation. Gives some do's and don'ts. Briefly summarizes the project histories from the participants in the Northern Rockies Program on Women in the Curriculum. Reviews projects aimed at reforming general education (University of Wyoming, Western Wyoming College, and Lewis-Clark State College, Idaho); faculty development (Central Wyoming State, Southern Utah Sate College, and the University of Utah); networking/consortial efforts (University of Idaho/Washington State, and University of Montana); and expanding options for women students (Montana College of Mineral Science and Technology and Weber State). Includes an annotated bibliography of general works, background readings, course revision models by field, project evaluations, and other resources.

292.    Schoem, David, and others, eds. *Multicultural Teaching in the University.* Westport, CT: Praeger Publishers, 1993. 362 pp.

Divides the chapters into eight parts: (1) an introduction to the meaning of multicultural teaching; (2) courses on intergroup relations (e.g., teaching with and about conflict, a framework for teaching Latinos in the United States, and recollections on the teaching of multicultural courses); (3) courses on racism, sexism, and diversity (e.g., anti-racism and multiculturalism in a law school class, multicultural teaching in public health, and lesbian studies and multicultural teaching); (4) general courses that give attention to diversity (e.g., teaching mathematics to minorities, racial bias in science education, a multicultural approach to writing, a white male teaches social inequality and oppression, and social psychology); (5) teacher training and nonformal education (e.g., the use of dialogue groups, faculty development on issues of racism and diversity, and a teaching-assistant training program with a multicultural emphasis); (6) a roundtable discussion on the insiders' critique of multicultural teaching; (7) questions and responses on multicultural teaching and conflict in the classroom; and (8) classroom and workshop exercises. Also includes a selected bibliography.

293.   Spanier, Bonnie, Alexander Bloom, and Darlene Boroviak, eds. *Toward A Balanced Curriculum: A Sourcebook for Initiating Gender Integration Projects*. Cambridge, MA: Schenkman Publishing Company, Inc., 1984. 364 pp.

Generated from the 1983 Wheaton College Conference on the integration of the study of women into the college curriculum. Divides the discussion into four parts: (1) conference proceedings (e.g., disciplinary development, interactive phases of curricular revision, redefining the humanities canon, establishing gender as a category in the social sciences, the concept of *objectivity* in the natural sciences, institutional models of curriculum change, the partnership of black studies and women's studies, location of resources, and support and assessment); (2) transforming courses (definitions/guidelines and changes within the disciplines: art history, biology, chemistry, education, English, history, music, political science, psychology, and sociology); (3) bibliographies, resources, and other projects (e.g., an initial reading in feminist theory, the new research integrated into economics, feminist critiques of the natural and social sciences, black women's studies and women and American government); and (4) projects of conference participants (project descriptions and guidelines).

294.    Stafford, Beth, ed. *Directory of Women's Studies Programs &*
        *Library Resources*. Phoenix, AZ: Oryx Press, 1990. 154 pp.

        Includes the results of 2 separate surveys conducted in
        1987 and 1988 of more than 2,000 U.S. institutions of higher
        education. Encompasses both programs and courses with
        each entry including school and/or program name, address,
        contact person, and telephone number. Frequently also
        includes teaching faculty, other teaching affiliates, courses
        offered, degree(s) offered, certificates(s) offered, library
        contact person(s), library support services and special
        resources. Also presents four specific indexes: institution,
        women's studies credentials, discipline orientation, and
        library collection subject strength.

295.    Taylor, Charles A., ed. *Guide to Multicultural Resources*
        *1993/1994*. Madison, WI: Praxis Publications, Inc. 1993. 474
        pp.

        Serves as a directory, mediagraphy, and almanac on
        multicultural organizations, services, and trends. Includes
        lists of African-, Asian-, Hispanic-, and Native-American
        associations, institutions, organizations, and other entities.
        Also includes local, state, and federal governmental agencies
        that have multicultural agendas. Arranged into five major
        sections: African-American, Hispanic-American, Asian-
        American, Native-American, and multicultural American
        resources. Divides each of these into the categories of, for
        example, arts/cultural organizations, colleges and
        universities, educational organizations/resources, libraries
        and bookstores, museums and historical societies, and
        women's organizations. Also includes for each section an
        introductory essay and pertinent selected statistics, plus six
        indexes: organization, subject, geographic, index of
        executives, publications, and video.

296.    Tierney, Helen, ed. *Women's Studies Encyclopedia*, 3 vols. New
        York: Greenwood Press, 1989, 1990, and 1991.

Is divided into three separate subtitled volumes: Views from the Sciences (volume 1, 1989, 417 pp.), Literature, Arts, and Learning (volume 2, 1990, 381 pp.), and History, Philosophy, and Religion (volume 3, 1991, 531 pp.). Presents in each volume contributions from major thinkers and writers in the disparate areas that contribute to courses in women's studies. All three are alphabetically arranged and include separate selected bibliographies and lists of both consultants and contributors with their professional affiliations.

297. Tulloch, Paulette P., and Susan A. Hallgarth. *A Directory of National Women's Organizations.* New York: National Council for Research on Women, 1992. 664 pp.

Provides a comprehensive alphabetical list of women's organizations and organizations with women's committees or commissions. Includes contact person, description of the organization, areas of focus, services offered, publications, user access, target population, and meeting information. Presents a useful guide to educational professional associations and their specific efforts (e.g., American Sociological Association's Commission on the Status of Women and American Association for Higher Education-Women's Caucus). Gives a listing of centers for the study of women (e.g., Barnard College, Duke University, Memphis State, and Wellesley). Also provides a keyword index covering specific topics of interest (e.g., curriculum transformation, cultural diversity, curriculum integration, women's studies, higher education, gender issues, and multicultural issues).

298. Urban Community Colleges Commission. *Minorities in Urban Community Colleges: Tomorrow's Students Today.* Washington, DC: American Association of Community and Junior Colleges, 1988. 29 pp.

Presents in a monograph an analysis of the trends in minority enrollment in urban community colleges, and explores issues of recruitment and retention of minority students, program choice, transfer and articulation, and support services for students. Includes such specific subtopics as major fields of study, degrees, financial aid, academic preparation, sociocultural adjustment, minority-student transfer to four-year baccalaureate institutions, program and curriculum development, community linkages, and research.

299.    Whaley, Sara Stauffer, editor/publisher. *Women (sic) Studies Abstracts*. New Brunswick, N.J.: Transaction Periodicals Consortium, Rutgers University. Published quarterly.

Presents journal abstracts in an extensive set of categories, including women's studies; education and socialization; society; religion, philosophy, and ethics; literature, media, theater and films; biography and criticism; and book reviews. Includes in all editions an annual index in the fourth issue (from vol. 13).

300.    Women's Studies Librarian. *A Guide to Nonprint Resources in Women's Studies: Coverage of Selected Titles 1985-1990*. Madison, WI: Women's Studies Librarian, University of Wisconsin System, n.d. 88 pp.

Lists and briefly annotates a selection of English-language films, radio productions, filmstrips, slide shows, and audio cassettes produced between 1985 and 1990. Divides into the categories of anthropology; art, architecture, photography, film, and music; biography, autobiography, diaries, and memoirs; economics, business and work; education; health, medicine, and biology; history; humor; international studies; journalism, mass communications, and publishing; language and linguistics; law; narrative works; poetry; politics and political theory; psychology; religion and spirituality; science and mathematics; sexuality; sociology and social issues; sports; and women's movement and feminist studies. Is indexed by both title and subject and includes an alphabetical list of distributors.

301. *Women's Studies Index*. Boston: G.K. Holland Co., Published yearly.

> Includes an extensive alphabetical listing of journal articles or reviews on a multitude of topics, issues, and disciplines related to women's studies. Also includes a list of periodicals indexed and their addresses.

302. "Women's Studies Programs – 1994." *Women's Studies Quarterly* 22 (1 & 2) (Spring/Summer 1994):141-175.

> Gives a current list of women's studies programs nationwide, maintained as an educational service by *Women's Studies Quarterly*. Provides addresses, contact people, and types of educational offerings: traditional degrees, concentration, certificate, minor, graduate concentration, graduate certificate, and graduate minor.

# APPENDIX
# ALPHABETICAL LISTING
# OF REFERENCED JOURNALS

Academe
American Behavioral Scientist
American Quarterly
Art Education
Change
College Composition and Communication
College English
College Teaching
Communication Education
Counselors
Education and Urban Society
Education for Social Work
Educational Research
Educational Review
Educational Studies in Mathematics
Feminist Issues
Feminist Studies
Feminist Teacher
Harvard Educational Review
Initiatives
Journal of American Indian Education
Journal of Black Studies
Journal of Education
Journal of Multilingual and Multicultural Development
Journal of the National Association for Women Deans, Administrators, and Counselors
Journal of Negro Education
Journal of Social Work Education
Liberal Education
Multicultural Review
Music Educators Journal
NASPA Journal
New Directions for Teaching and Learning
Reference Services Review

Signs: Journal of Women in Culture and Society
Teachers College Record
Teaching Sociology
The Chronicle of Higher Education
The College Board Review
The Journal of American History
The Journal of Academic Librarianship
The Journal of General Education
The Journal of Higher Education
The Negro Educational Review
The Public Interest
The Social Studies
The University of Georgia Research Reporter
The Western Journal of Black Studies
Urban Anthropology
Women's Studies in Communication
Women's Studies Quarterly

# AUTHOR INDEX

(This author index is listed alphabetically. The numbers refer to the annotation number.)

# Source Books on Education

**SCHOOL PLAY**
*A Source Book*
by James H. Block
and Nancy R. King

**ADULT LITERACY**
*A Source Book and Guide*
by Joyce French

**BLACK CHILDREN AND
AMERICAN INSTITUTIONS**
*An Ecological Review and
Resource Guide*
by Valora Washington
and Velma LaPoint

**SEXUALITY EDUCATION**
*A Resource Book*
by Carol Cassell
and Pamela M. Wilson

**REFORMING TEACHER
EDUCATION**
*Issues and New Directions*
edited by Joseph A. Braun, Jr.

**CRITICAL ISSUES IN FOREIGN
LANGUAGE INSTRUCTION**
edited by Ellen S. Silber

**THE EDUCATION OF WOMEN
IN THE UNITED STATES**
*A Guide to Theory, Teaching,
and Research*
by Averil Evans McClelland

**MATERIALS AND STRATEGIES
FOR THE EDUCATION
OF TRAINABLE MENTALLY
RETARDED LEARNERS**
by James P. White

**EDUCATIONAL TESTING**
*Issues and Applications*
by Kathy E. Green

**TEACHING THINKING SKILLS**
*Theory and Practice*
by Joyce N. French
and Carol Rhoder

**TEACHING SOCIAL STUDIES
TO THE YOUNG CHILD**
*A Research and Resource Guide*
by Blythe S. Farb Hinitz

**TELECOMMUNICATIONS**
*A Handbook for Educators*
by Reza Azarmsa

**SECONDARY SCHOOLS
AND COOPERATIVE LEARNING**
*Theories, Models, and Strategies*
edited by Jon E. Pederson
and Annette D. Digby

**SCHOOL PRINCIPALS AND CHANGE**
by Michael D. Richardson,
Paula M. Short,
and Robert L. Prickett

**PLAY IN PRACTICE**
*A Systems Approach to Making
Good Play Happen*
edited by Karen VanderVen,
Paul Niemiec,
and Roberta Schomburg

**TEACHING SCIENCE TO
CHILDREN**
*Second Edition*
by Mary D. Iatridis with a
contribution by Miriam Maracek

**KITS, GAMES AND MANIPULATIVES
FOR THE ELEMENTARY SCHOOL
CLASSROOM**
*A Source Book*
by Andrea Hoffman
and Ann Glannon